"Rupert Ashe has created a succinct, readab[] honest guide to the realities of selling a m[] huge depth of experience comes through knowledge he shares and the advice he gi[] close as you will get to a manual for the successful acquisiti[].[] agency.

Nothing is quite as scary for the entrepreneur as the acquisition process; having mastered your marketing discipline over many years, established a great client base and built up a really great agency you are suddenly plunged into a void of ignorance. This book demystifies the strange metamorphosis of an agency going through an acquisition and calmly leads your thinking through a process that seems simultaneously capable of delivering your greatest dreams and manifesting your worst fears."
Julian Tanner, Founder and CEO, Acxicom (a subsidiary of WPP PLC)

"Selling my agency is probably the most stressful thing I have ever done (it beats marriage, divorce, having kids and moving house hands down!). Building a business is a deeply personal thing to do – very similar to having a child – it's born and then you watch it grow up and become strong and you take enormous pride in its achievements. To then put it up for adoption is a wrench to say the least! Having a good advisor is the core of steel that keeps the deal between buyer and seller sane. Impartial advice, focus on what's important, identification of 'deal breakers' plus many more benefits can be found in a good advisor. The book allows the seller to understand the needs of the buyer without the humiliation of constantly having to ask them dumb questions. Rupert's book would have been gold dust in the time leading up to the sale of my company (and certainly would have saved me some of the fees I paid him!). Reading it seven years after I sold my company, I felt a swell of pride that we managed between us to do an exemplary deal. So I guess he knows what he's talking about…"
Catherine Warne, Co-Founder and CEO, Red Door Communications Group (a subsidiary of Creston PLC)

"Rupert Ashe's book is essential reading for any aspiring entrepreneur in the world of marketing. The sale process is part art, part science and can be quite confusing, so being armed with as much knowledge as possible is a pre-requisite to a good outcome. Selling an agency successfully is not easy; if you are out-of-step in any part of the choreography, you can fall down and lose value. Being mentally prepared and with the right advisors at hand will make the process as painless as possible."

James Hilton, Co-Founder and Joint Managing Director, M&C Saatchi Mobile (a subsidiary of M&C Saatchi PLC)

"When selling your company, you need your guardian angel at your side to guide you through the complex, lengthy and stressful process. This book is vital reading for any owner of an agency looking to sell. It provides a solid base of understanding so that you can appoint the right adviser, find the right buyer and achieve the right result."

Liz Shanahan, Senior Managing Director, FTI Strategic Communications

ABOUT THE AUTHOR

Rupert Ashe is a corporate financier and entrepreneur. After graduating from Bristol University, he qualified as a Chartered Accountant while working with Deloitte in London. After a period in the Deloitte Corporate Finance Department, he left to establish a communications training business in the City of London, which in 1991 he subsequently merged to form Focus Communications, a financial PR and investor relations agency. As Chief Executive of Focus Communications he advised on over fifty flotations and mergers and acquisitions before selling the agency to Grey Global Group in 1997, where he became Head of the Global Financial Practice of GCI Group. In 2002 he established Wall House Consulting, a strategic consultancy, which acted on over thirty M&A and fund-raising transactions in the media and marketing services sectors. In 2011 he sold Wall House Consulting to D5 Capital (UK) Limited, a corporate finance adviser. As a Director of D5 Capital he is responsible for agency sales and acquisitions, as well as conducting fund-raising activities for start-up companies, and is regulated by the FSA as an Appointed Representative of Bristol York Limited. During his career, Rupert has acted as Chief Financial Officer in a number of start-up companies in media and marketing services and taken those companies through their eventual trade sales, so he has experience of the sale process as adviser and as principal. He lives in London with his wife Jackie and their two children, Isabel and Marcus.

MAKING MILLIONS FROM CREATIVITY:

How to sell a marketing services agency

Financial freedom from the sale of a 'people' business

RUPERT ASHE

First published in Great Britain in 2012
by Wall House Publications, 53 Chandos Place, London WC2N 4HS
Rupert@d5capital.com

Matador
9 Priory Business Park,
Wistow Road, Kibworth Beauchamp,
Leicestershire. LE8 0RX
Tel: (+44) 116 279 2299
Fax: (+44) 116 279 2277
Email: books@troubador.co.uk
Web: www.troubador.co.uk/matador

ISBN 978 1780882 611

British Library Cataloguing in Publication Data.
A catalogue record for this book is available from the British Library.

Typeset by Troubador Publishing Ltd, Leicester, UK

Matador is an imprint of Troubador Publishing Ltd.

Printed and bound in the UK by TJ International, Padstow, Cornwall

This book is dedicated to Jackie, who was my partner in business when we sold our agency all those years ago and is my partner in life today.

ACKNOWLEDGEMENTS

I would like to thank Nick Taylor, Head of Corporate at Higgs & Sons Solicitors for his guidance on legal protocol, particularly in Chapter 12 and the Glossary – much appreciated, Nick!

CONTENTS

1 Introduction   1

2 Agencies are special businesses   3

3 Reasons to sell your agency   12

4 Anatomy of a buyer   17

5 Getting ready to sell   20

6 The approach   26

7 Advisers: whom to use and what to pay them   34

8 Talking to buyers: the negotiation   36

9 The Heads of Terms   45

10 Earn-Outs   50

11 Due diligence (DD)   55

12 Sale and Purchase Agreement (SPA)   60

13 Completion   67

14 Partial sales and all-paper mergers   72

15 Disputes   77

16 Conclusion   78

Appendix: Glossary of terms   79

CHAPTER ONE:
Introduction

This book is primarily aimed at the entrepreneur agency owner in the marketing services sector, with a particular emphasis on the United Kingdom. After all the years of sweat and toil, developing services, winning clients, keeping clients and holding on to talented staff, the day of reckoning comes: the decision to sell the agency. Because many entrepreneurs only sell once and usually to serial Buyers, the process is generally alien and the disparity between their knowledge of the deal and that of the Buyer is often considerable. Having gone through the process of company disposal many times, both as a principal and as an adviser, I am acutely aware that the transaction can only be optimised for the Sellers if they are fully engaged in the process and make use of all the acquired wisdom that they can lay their hands on. It is not a time for improvisation.

This book aims to de-mystify the process, to consider the respective motivations of both Buyer and Seller and arm the Seller with sufficient knowledge to interact with and manage his/her advisers and to play the appropriate role in the transaction. The outcome of 'the transaction' should be financial reward for the Seller's flair and a successful operating business (in perpetuity) for the Buyer. In the creative services industry, this is often difficult to achieve. Agencies are reliant on people and knowledge, both highly mobile assets. Harnessing those elements once the original mission is complete takes a very particular skill and demands certain structures that have evolved as the bigger agency groups have perfected their craft.

Although this book is primarily aimed at owners of advertising agencies and networks, branding consultancies, communications consultancies, design agencies, digital marketing businesses, direct marketing agencies, marketing data analysis businesses, market research companies, mobile advertising agencies and all the plethora of specialisations in the marketing services industry, many of the lessons learned can be applied to the sale of people businesses in other corporate service sectors.

The book aims to be a 'nuts and bolts' analysis of the pre-sale and sale process where I have spent most of my career providing advice and guidance. What I do not seek to analyse in detail are the integration processes conducted by the Buyer post Completion for there are many more worthy texts on this subject, which provide the Buyer's perspective on methods for taking agencies on to the next level of excellence, long after the agencies' creators have left. What I would say, however, is that the real success of mergers and acquisitions in this creative industry lies in a true partnership between Buyer and Seller: they must work together to create a shared vision of the future and ensure that all the team involved in the business post acquisition – and that includes the Sellers in most instances – are as motivated and excited by their work and their rewards as they were in the early years of the agency. This partnership demands that both sides are absolutely clear on what each expects of the other and that both parties behave with the utmost integrity in their dealings. If agencies succeed in (at least) the first five years post acquisition, everyone gains: the Buyer has a flourishing business and a strong possibility of a positive return on their original investment; the Seller has a successful Earn-Out (being the additional capital payment(s) made based on the company's post-acquisition performance) and a far greater chance of continuing in the agency after the completion of that Earn-Out.

Needless to say, this book is merely a condensed overview from one person of a complex and detailed subject matter. There are infinite variations and peculiarities in every deal that require special treatment and advice. If you want to discuss any issue as it affects your own agency, or debate any of my conclusions, please feel free to drop me a line:

Rupert@d5capital.com

CHAPTER TWO:
Agencies are special businesses

A particularly suave and longstanding communications entrepreneur once told me that all one needed to start an agency was 'a telephone and a decent dining room table'. Although the professionalism of new agencies has leapt ahead in the past thirty years as the digital age has gripped the world of marketing services, the central premise of his quip remains valid. The agency world is one that is constantly spawning exciting start-ups, as executives spot better ways of serving the corporate world. These only require small amounts of capital to create but large amounts of inspiration and perspiration to grow.

Perpetual consolidation
It is also a world of perpetual consolidation; big agencies are always gobbling up smaller ones. And smaller agencies are created every day. A Google search reveals that there are over 12,000 advertising-related companies, 8,000 marketing agencies, 1,000 PR agencies, and hundreds of digital marketing agencies in the UK alone. It is a massively fragmented industry in terms of sheer numbers of participants, although client spending is quite concentrated in the hands of the leading agency groups. Talented management teams can break away and rapidly develop a client base if they have something new and exciting to offer. This is often what catches the eye of the large agency groups that come knocking on their doors.

Typically, there are seven buyer categories that may be interested in buying your marketing services/marketing technology agency:

• Global players: direct purchases by the major global holding companies with cash resources to buy throughout the business cycle. The major marketing services groups are Dentsu, Omnicom,

Publicis Groupe, and WPP. Others that are active but with smaller balance sheets include Havas, Hakuhodo and Interpublic Group (IPG). The media giants that are seeking to acquire interesting marketing services technologies also fall into this category, including groups such as Apple, AOL, Facebook, Google, Microsoft, Yahoo! and Scripps.

- Brands within global players: a study of the acquisitions by the global players in recent years will show that the acquiring vehicle is often one of the existing brands of the holding company – such as TNS, Kantar, Burson Marsteller and Ogilvy at WPP.
- Smaller listed groups: these include companies such as Aegis, Chime, Creston, Huntsworth, M&C Saatchi, Mission Marketing, Next Fifteen, Porta Communications, YouGov and others. Overseas markets such as Australia and Canada develop their own consolidation vehicles which acquire in the UK, with varying degrees of success.
- Marketing technology and digital marketing groups: increasingly fast growing marketing technology and digital groups, usually listed on NASDAQ, have a view to growing internationally. These include both digital marketing services giants such as ValueClick and marketing technology developers such as Acxicom.
- Private equity backed 'buy and build' vehicles that aim to consolidate a range of agencies during a cyclical up-turn before exiting via a trade sale or a flotation.
- Private companies in the UK and US, using their retained earnings, bank finance and high net worth individual's equity investment to make acquisitions.
- Management Buy Out/In: Second-tier management backed by private equity/venture capital trusts; serial entrepreneurs seeking to buy into a smaller agency and repeat their former success.

A valuable insight into the motivations of Buyers is provided annually by media specialist Admedia Partners, the market leading advisory partnership based in the US. In their Annual Survey (January 2012) Admedia Partners found in response to the question as to what would drive their M&A activities in 2012, 63% cited the need to develop a new product/service offering and 56% cited the development of new clients and new verticals. Global expansion was cited by 31%. This shows that the main driver of M&A is effective portfolio management: by product/service, by industry vertical and by geography. All acquirers want to be plugged into areas of growth.

Global players

A review of the 2011 regulatory announcements of the listed marketing services groups that are active buyers in the UK indicated that – even in a quiet period for mergers and acquisitions globally – as a group they made 94 acquisitions across 24 countries of which 81% were made by the global players, either directly or through one of their major sub-brands. The dominant themes were expansion in the 'BRICs' countries (Brazil, Russia, India and China) and the deepening of digital marketing capabilities in the USA and Europe. In spite of the UK's record of slower economic growth than in most of the other 24 countries, no less than 13 of the 94 deals were carried out in the UK. As far as marketing services are concerned, the UK remains a large, mature market with a good track record for innovation. Inevitably, the lack of confidence in the UK's stock markets (London Stock Exchange (LSE), Alternative Investment Market (AIM) and PLUS) meant that the main buyers were those with substantial cash resources and which had no need to seek additional funding from investors to complete deals, such as Dentsu (listed on the Tokyo Stock Exchange), Publicis Groupe (listed on EuroNext), Omnicom (listed on the New York Stock Exchange (NYSE)) and WPP (listed on the LSE and NYSE).

It is worth mentioning that for developers of marketing platforms and advertising technology, the universe of potential buyers extends to the media and technology giants such as Apple, Google and Microsoft in the US, data services groups such as Experian in the UK and emerging advertising network players such as Adconion. Recent deals in digital and mobile advertising networks (the acquisitions of Admob and Quattro) and Facebook advertising platforms (Techlightenment) illustrate this trend.

Brands within global players

Where a major player elects to make the acquisition through one of its global brands, this will mean that the decision-making process can become more complex, because line management of the sub-brand and central corporate finance teams will be involved (plus regional general management in some cases). This should not be a problem as long as the Seller appreciates the respective roles of all interested parties during the transaction. The sub-brand management will be primarily concerned with the operational fit and the detailed due diligence searches on the people, clients and profits. They will be less involved with (although highly impacted by) the pricing and structuring of the payments to the Sellers, as this is the domain of the central corporate finance team who will be responsible for the funding of the deal and the presentation of the transaction to institutional investors.

Smaller listed groups

Smaller listed consolidation groups are primarily pro-cyclical, as they require access to fresh equity capital and bank debt to make significant acquisitions.

Listed UK groups remain important buyers of UK agencies, although their appetite to acquire in the UK varies depending on their existing strength in specific disciplines in the UK and their ability to raise capital. In recent years, the UK agency groups have been seeking to diversify overseas; nevertheless they are still keen buyers in the UK where they need additional capabilities, either by vertical industry sector (for example in healthcare, technology, financial services, sports etc.) or by skill set (mobile advertising, data analysis, advertising networks, customer re-targeting etc.). In addition, there is a range of listed companies headquartered in US, Canada, Europe and Australia which have made forays into the UK, with differing degrees of success. Examples include the Canadian group Cossette that acquired Band & Brown and the Australian Photon Group which acquired Frank PR and Hotwire in the UK. Deals by the smaller UK-listed vehicles often (but not always) include a share element. Typically, negotiations will open at a 50:50 split of cash and shares, although this will often end up closer to 75:25 cash and shares. Over the years, this segment has witnessed the greatest volatility, as players over-extended themselves by using debt to partly finance acquisitions which themselves contained substantial Earn-Outs. This 'double whammy' has led to some high profile collapses in the past, such as Cordiant Communications (one-time owner of Saatchi & Saatchi) which was eventually split into two parts and absorbed by Publicis and WPP. Other recent demises include Media Square plc who bought 16 businesses from Hunstworth in 2005 for £63m and subsequently went into administration at the end of 2011, and Adventis plc which peaked at 70p in early 2007 and is now suspended from AIM.

Private equity backed buy and build vehicles

As far as private equity is concerned, the marketing services sector has always been an attractive target market for those seeking to 'buy and build' due to the fact that the sector is cash generative and fragmented. Examples of the model include Advent International's acquisition, development and eventual sale of FD (formerly Financial Dynamics) to FTI Consulting, listed on NYSE. HIG Capital's backing of Engine Group and Vitruvian Partners' backing of the College Group, are more recent examples. Private equity buyers tend to seek businesses with solid cash flow that can support a degree of leverage as this can greatly enhance the eventual return to equity holders. Deals tend to therefore be financed with cash (with small amounts of equity sometimes available in the earlier deals). The other key factor for the seller to consider is that any 'roll-up' vehicle (a specially created holding group for acquiring companies, often supported by private equity) will seek an exit within the standard 5–7 year timeframe from the initial investment. Thus the selling entrepreneur must be aware that his/her Earn-Out should fit within that timeframe.

Private companies

When selling to a private company, the structures adopted will be the more cautious owing to the fact that the Buyers may be more capital-constrained in comparison to their listed counterparts. Thus acquisitions are likely to involve significant minority shareholdings retained by the entrepreneur, Deferred Consideration and the use of Vendor Loan Notes. In such instances, there will be a greater demand for compelling post acquisition synergies, as the Seller will be joining a 'family' of companies that will be targeting an eventual joint exit. However, these unlisted groups can provide very satisfactory exits for agencies that need help in growing through central management services and greater marketing clout. The main issue, however, is to control the risk profile of the transaction by avoiding too large an element of Deferred Consideration. It is also incumbent on the Seller to conduct a greater degree of investigative 'reverse' due diligence on the Buyer, as they will not have the comfort of substantial balance sheets to underpin future payments. Examples of emerging private acquisition vehicles are Four Communications Group, Gyro, Lansons Communications and Writtle Holdings.

Management Buy-Outs

A Management Buy-Out (MBO) tends not to be the preferred route in the marketing services sector and MBOs tend to occur when a holding company decides to dispose of unwanted assets rather than when an entrepreneur seeks to sell up. The Vendor Initiated Management Buy-Out (VIMBO) can be quite difficult to pull off at a decent price, for a variety of reasons. The first is that relatively few entrepreneur-led agencies have second-tier management that is able (or indeed willing) to persuade a private equity provider or business angel to back the Management Buy-Out. Without ready access to equity capital, the management team is left seeking finance from (a) banks (b) themselves (c) the Company or (d) the Vendor. As a result, the price achieved is usually heavily discounted from what a Seller would hope to achieve on a trade sale. The flip side is that the deal process can be shorter as both sides understand the business and the consideration is usually paid in cash or some form of Vendor Loan Note issued by the company which can be re-paid from future profits, bank loans or equity injections. For a retiring Seller, this can be appealing as the deal can be structured in a tax efficient manner and their withdrawal from the company can be gradual as their Loan Notes are redeemed.

The main risk of the MBO is that if management does not want to 'step up to the plate', it is effectively a signal that they do not want to be company owners – or worse, that they can envisage being company owners, but not at the relatively high entry cost of the MBO. Because succession management forms a large part of the goodwill of the company, the negotiating power can transfer rapidly away from the Seller during an MBO, with unfortunate consequences. The main protection against this happening, as always, is price tension through the possible sale of the agency to a trade buyer. Those MBOs that have succeeded have always had the same ingredients: a capable and ambitious second-tier management layer, a mature agency and founders that are supportive of the process and of the agency post Completion.

Intangible asset value is the key to valuation
What this means is that the value of the typical agency is usually mostly intangible: management know-how, client relationships and contracts, brand reputation and creative energy. In some cases, agencies can develop harder assets such as technology platforms, data analysis tools or other valuable intellectual property, but in most cases, the value of the agency 'goes up and down in the lift' on a daily basis, so it takes particular skill to distil that into a successful company disposal.

Focus on founders
The fortunes of even the biggest companies in the world can be traced to the leadership of key individuals (anyone that doubts this can analyse the impact of Steve Jobs or Bill Gates on the value of Apple and Microsoft during their tenures), so it is little wonder that the structures developed for buying agencies are all about *harnessing great management talent.* Very few Buyers of agencies want to see the agency management walking out of the Completion Meeting with their swimming trunks/swimsuit on. As the industry has developed, so the sophistication of the best Buyers in the industry has blossomed. Today, better organised, better structured Buyers have a great track record in management retention. Some of the most successful agency sales of all time have seen the selling management stay with the Buyer for many years after the deal was done.

'Crossroad' moments for agencies

But, at certain points in the lifecycle of an agency, this intangible value can become brittle:

- in the early years, when agencies are dependent on certain, major clients;
- at the point where the founders are no longer managing the major client relationships;
- when the agency decides to expand overseas;
- when the founders start the process of management succession to the next generation.

These are key moments when value can be multiplied or lost, depending on the skill of execution.

A frequently-asked question is 'When should a management team sell an agency to get the best value?' It is an impossible one to answer empirically, as everyone has a different view of the vocational value of their agency and different levels of management skill required to drive forward a larger and larger agency group. But there are certain central 'laws' that should be respected in working out when to sell.

The first is to accept that most agencies **under expert and energetic leadership** will continue to grow, so the longer you hold on to the asset, the bigger the ultimate realisation, assuming that the founders continue to learn and improve. The second point is that the words 'expert and energetic' are important; if the agency has outgrown your ability to manage it, or you have lost personal momentum, then succession must occur either via a sale or by installing new management. If an agency does not constantly re-invent itself, it will grow old and tired and ultimately go 'ex-growth'.

The third is that you will attract a higher multiple (of annual profits) if you are sufficiently big and still growing. It will come as no surprise that agencies with an exciting growth product/service or who are operating in fast-growth niches will attract most attention from acquirers. This 'gold rush' effect has been seen many times in the acquisition of online advertising networks, digital agencies, mobile marketing agencies, healthcare communications consultancies and social networking specialists. So it is definitely worth accepting that in the period prior to a disposal, to have one or more exciting (and profitable) 'growth' services emerging will add value. Also, if your annual pre-tax profits are less than £1m, you may be considered 'sub-scale' by the larger Buyers. Mounting a takeover of an agency will cost the Buyer a minimum of £50,000–£100,000 in professional fees and management time irrespective of the size of the target, so smaller businesses will simply not be cost effective, nor will they make a material impact on the group profit and loss to warrant the effort.

The fourth point to remember is that no one wants to provide a retirement fund for agency-owners. If much of the value in an agency is tied to the contacts and skills of founders that are approaching retirement age, then value will begin to drain away unless high quality succession management has arrived in the board room. In one instance, a majority shareholder/proprietor close to retirement age announced to a prospective Buyer that he was only prepared to do one year with the agency post acquisition. In US football parlance, it was a 'yellow flag on the field of play'.

Finally, you must be aware of the business cycle. Although we were raised on the notion that business cycles are seven years in length, this concept is no longer reliable folklore. Ask the business community in Japan, who have been locked in a seemingly never-ending bear market. Picking your moment is now a harder decision. The ideal is to have positive trading conditions for the two years prior and three to five years post Completion, which indicates that a sale in early to mid cycle is preferable, so that you can experience a happy Earn-Out.

CHAPTER THREE:
Reasons to sell your agency

Admiring glances
There is nothing more attractive to a Buyer than an agency that has no intention of selling.

In the same way that Groucho Marx once wrote in a resignation note 'I don't care to belong to any club that would have me as a member', so Buyers don't want to acquire agencies where the owners are just waiting to cash in their chips. That doesn't mean that you can't initiate the process – it simply means that you wait for the best possible moment of choice while you build value into your agency.

If you look at the hundreds of agency sales that have been completed over the past 25 years in the UK, it would be fair to say that – in the majority of cases, excluding major advertising agency/network sales – the sums involved were less than £50m and probably most of those involved payments of less than £20m, usually shared between a handful of founders. Therefore the conclusion must be that in each case the sale transaction provided financial security for the founders, rather than Warren Buffet-style wealth. At a more prosaic level, disposal is often a way of providing for retirement, allowing time for an adequate period of post-acquisition integration.

It is also fair to say that in most cases, the Seller of an agency sees commercial advantages from being part of something bigger. Usually this is the 'network effect', whereby clients can be referred from/to overseas colleagues or introduced to specialist services that the selling agency can't offer. Whether or not this is a mirage is difficult to track as agency owners are often tight-lipped during an Earn-Out period, for obvious reasons. But anecdotal evidence from agencies that I have acted for indicates that the 'multiple profit centre'/'silo' structure of most large agency groups makes collegiate behaviour complex and Sellers are often disappointed in these promised 'revenue synergies'. One agency owner told me that he believed that joining an international group would be like riding a sled with a hundred huskies pulling him along; only to find that he was one of the huskies pulling the sled... which was being driven by the Group CEO!

Timeline to disposal

The best way to work out a disposal timeline is to work back from a date in the future when you want to stop doing the business of your agency – either to do something else or to do nothing but lie on a beach. This is the end of your post-integration period or Earn-Out and can be up to five years after the date that you sell the agency.

Then count back to the date of sale. At this point, you should be as attractive a purchase as you will ever be: fast-growing, profitable, well-managed and with an exciting plan for expansion.

Then, count back a further year to allow for the sale process to be completed. It may take less time, but allow a year.

Then count back *again* another 2 years to enable you to prepare the business for sale and establish a track record of rising profits. That is the point where you are firing the starting pistol on your sale. It all adds up, doesn't it? In essence, it is at least a business cycle, if not longer. In total, you may be looking at up to 8 years for the whole plan to unfold, taking no account of extraneous factors such as recessions, which may stretch the timeline. Now clearly, this timeline can move much faster for 'rocket' agencies which hit the zeitgeist and grow at break-neck speed for three to four years before being snapped up. But for most businesses, the process from beginning to end is an economic cycle.

The next step is to work out what will make the agency an attractive purchase. And then try and deliver that story.

Attributes for a strategic purchase or bolt-on acquisition
So what are acquirers looking for? It varies enormously, but if you consider preferred Buyers – those with access to substantial cash resources, usually listed on public markets or backed by substantial private equity interests – they usually all have certain fixed investment criteria. These will vary depending on whether you are a 'must have/strategic' purchase or a 'bolt-on/nice-to-have' purchase. The former tend to be larger deals that bring a new skills set into the group and are maintained as a stand-alone brand. The latter are usually designed to bolster a core subsidiary brand of the Buyer's group and tend to be subsumed into that sub-brand.

The criteria for a strategic, 'must-have' purchase would be as follows:

(a) Substantial: >£5m income and >£1m Earnings Before Interest and Tax (EBIT);
(b) Profitable: 20%+ Net Margin before tax;
(c) Growing: annual growth in EBIT of 10%;
(d) Market leadership: top ten player in chosen discipline and location/city, award-winning, high profile;
(e) Scalability: ability to grow profits by factor of 2 or 3 times over first five years of ownership;
(f) Dynamic management: talented management team that is capable of leading the business for many years/able to act as 'rainmakers' for winning large client mandates in their chosen segment.

A 'bolt-on' would have less demanding criteria:

(a) Profitable: EBIT of £250k–£1m and net margin of >15%;
(b) Cash generative: consistent/improving profit delivery over the past 5 years (allowing for cyclical downturns);
(c) Definable franchise: clear specialisation that will add value or complement the acquiring subsidiary of the group;
(d) Reputable: good industry reputation (award-winning);
(e) Synergistic: ability to integrate into acquiring company;
(f) Dedicated management: a management team that is keen to continue to work for the business and ensure a smooth integration.

The above criteria give a clear indication of what Buyers are looking for.

First and foremost, they want profit and cash flow; without this, it is very difficult to pay agency owners cash up front, unless the agency delivers a cutting edge service that they can offer all their clients, or the scalability of the offering is irresistible (as with the mobile advertising network purchases by Apple, Microsoft and Google, for example). In addition, profits allow Buyers to achieve 'Multiple Arbitrage': this means that they can pay the agency owners a multiple of EBIT that is substantially (up to 50%) less than the multiple accorded to their market capitalisation by the stock market. This makes the purchase immediately 'accretive', as analysts in the US describe it (which means delivering a positive impact on the Buyer's earnings per share in the first year post acquisition).

Second, Buyers ideally want growth: their financial payback models will usually factor in a variable rate of profits growth over five years, based on the historic run-rate of growth. Very few acquisition models that I have seen factor in a recession/profits decline; maybe this will change in these more uncertain times! This growth should allow the Buyer to achieve payback of the initial consideration from post-tax profits within the first 5 years.

Third, they want 'strategic fit'. This can come on many levels: coverage in a new city, complementary services, conflict brand capabilities or just plain cost synergies. Acquisition groups are focused very heavily on operating efficiencies: they all have substantial operating platforms – offices, technology platforms, brands, and central management – which need to be leveraged. Many an acquisition has been stimulated by the need to fill empty office space! This is all good news for the selling agency: 'beauty is in the eye of the beholder'. The key is to understand who will find your agency attractive and why; and what your profits could be once all the cost synergies have been squeezed out via integration. These are both central to your ultimate valuation in the eyes of the Buyer.

The final point to remember is that all acquisition groups are opportunistic as well as strategic; they respond to fashion (remember the feverish excitement over website developers in the dotcom boom? And today's excitement over mobile media experts?). This may enable Buyers to 'post-rationalise' the purchase of an asset against their strategic intentions, if they can get it at the right price.

CHAPTER FOUR:
Anatomy of a Buyer

I once read a quote by a genetic scientist in a newspaper article: 'Choose your parents wisely.' Unfortunately (or fortunately for mankind) we can't do that – just as well, as we would all end up with parents looking like Brad Pitt and Angelina Jolie, with the speed of Usain Bolt and the wealth of Mark Zuckerberg. But when selling an agency, you can (within reason) choose your parent company. So what do you want them to look like?

Check the balance sheet
From bitter experience, you want them to be wealthy. Buyers with substantial balance sheets are capable – and pre-conditioned – to pay market rates for assets. Not only does this ensure that you are paid properly for your agency *up front* (removing the risk of deferred consideration – see below), but the multiple will reflect a market valuation for your agency, as they will almost certainly be listed on a publicly traded stock market or backed by a major private equity group. In addition, you can have a better prospect (although this is not failsafe) of any Earn-Out payments as they fall due, because they have the theoretical ability to go back to the market/their private equity backer for more capital in order to fund these commitments. Nevertheless, even the mighty can fall and there have been numerous examples of publicly listed companies collapsing in the agency arena (Cordiant Communications and, more recently, Media Square to name two such casualties) as the double impact of a cyclical downturn and balance sheet debts and/or Earn-Out commitments crushed them. But you start from a much better place if the Buyer's covenant is good. The key is to know if the acquisition will require the issue of fresh equity to institutions or whether there is sufficient cash/bank facility to cover the transaction. If new equity is required, you will be at the mercy of the

market – as numerous Sellers (and their advisers) discovered in 2008 when the Lehmann Brothers collapse shut the equity markets for a period.

Risk of deferred consideration

In the event that you are purchased by a private company, however robust their financial status, they will tend to be capital-constrained and thus keen to defer elements of the initial valuation of your agency. In effect they will be trying, in part, to get you to pay for your own purchase. This inevitably makes such a sale less attractive, as you will be leaving a proportion of your business 'at risk' in the event they cannot pay you the deferred element of the purchase price in the future. You may also find that they would prefer to purchase a majority of your shares (usually 50.1–75%) and leave you with the minority as an incentive to carry on working hard. This is explored later, but is often less appealing than an Earn-Out.

Need for integrity

The next attribute that you want to see in your chosen 'parents' is integrity. You are going to have to work together, so you need to know that they will be honourable. This is simply a case of detailed reference-taking: ex-employees, previous acquisitions, clients, previous business partners. All can help you build up a picture of their behaviour over the years. Again, this is where the spotlight of public markets can be very helpful, for not only do results announcements and analyst reports reveal the full extent of their past financial engineering but they will also tend to be very careful about behaviour towards acquisitions that could negatively impact their drive for future acquisitions. With social media channels waiting and eager to carry any gossip on their misdemeanours, public companies tend to be very careful about handling their affairs in such sensitive areas. As a consolidator, a public spat with an acquisition's management can prove very unhelpful to its ambitions.

Benefits of a big group

The final attribute that can prove valuable is if they have something specific that you want, but cannot afford. This can be anything that will help you win business, keep staff, or make more profit. It could be an office in an overseas city or an operating unit. Whatever it is, you must carry out due diligence beforehand as to whether you will be able to *harness the asset to your advantage*; this will depend on the internal mechanics of the group, which will be more complex, the older it is. For example, if opening an office in Frankfurt is a major objective, then you must get to meet the country manager for Germany before you complete, and discuss openly whether that is possible, or whether the local management would resist such a strategy.

Caveat Venditor (Seller Beware)!

CHAPTER FIVE:
Getting ready to sell

All that glisters is not gold . . .
Imagine that you wake up on your birthday and you see a gleaming parcel at the foot of your bed. You grab it, pulse racing. You rip open the beautiful wrapping paper, to reveal a lovely white cardboard box containing a brand new gadget, with a pink bow tied round the middle. You untie it, open it and pull out the contents . . . only to find that several parts are missing, it has no battery, no power cable and the screen is cracked. How happy would you be then?

The same can happen in agency sales. Everyone is wildly excited at the outset – they like you, they like your shiny company and they like your growth record. And then they start digging . . . and all sorts of skeletons fly out of every cupboard. This is called due diligence and I look at it in more detail in Chapter 11. Negative due diligence can bring a sale grinding to a halt, so it is as well to understand the due diligence process and prepare your agency to pass the test with flying colours.

The process of due diligence tends to fall into two halves, one before signing Heads of Terms/Letter of Intent (which is quite limited) and the other half after signing the said Heads of Terms/Letter of Intent (which is very extensive). In essence, the Buyer is trying to find out if there are (a) any 'show-stoppers' that will prevent the deal from happening altogether; and (b) any specific areas of financial risk against which they need protection via warranties, indemnities and retentions.

Financial history
Before making an offer, any Buyer will want to dig around your historic financial and operational data. As a minimum, they will want to see:

- Growth: year-on-year movements in sales and profits (taking into account possible slowdowns in recessions);
- Margin: consistent margins (gross margin, margin after salaries, net margin after overheads);
- Spread of clients: no overdependence on individual clients;
- Quality clients: major brand names on the client list, showing that you are beginning to compete at the highest level;
- Technology: if you are a marketing technology developer, they will want to see that it works, is scalable and has successful reference sites;
- Client retention: ability to hold on to contracts, keep clients happy and expand client budgets;
- Staff retention: ability to hold on to talent and pay them market rates;
- Balance sheet ratios: ability to collect debtors and pay suppliers on time;
- Balance sheet strength: absence of long term bank debt or substantial overdrafts;
- Cash accumulation: ability to generate cash and pay dividends;
- Property commitments: ability to get out of onerous property commitments within a reasonable time period;
- Profitable offices: if you have regional or overseas offices, they should demonstrate emerging profitability;
- Directors' remuneration: the split of remuneration for founders/directors between salary and dividend, to assess the genuine profit delivery of the agency;
- Staff Incentives: nature of on-going staff incentives/options/management 'promises' to assess how the sale will affect the motivation of key staff;
- Tax: correct treatment of employee payments for income tax and an absence of aggressive tax planning schemes for the owners.

The simple fact is that private companies develop personal habits, so the longer you trade, the more likely it is that there will be idiosyncrasies in your operations that may well jar with a more institutionalised Buyer. Some agency owners tend to regard their businesses as a 'moneybox' extension of their personal financial lives and the line between personal and corporate can become somewhat blurred. While Buyers accept that proprietors will seek to minimise taxation – most usually (and legitimately) via the payment of dividends as opposed to large salaries and bonuses – they will seek to 'normalise' the profit trend to take this into account, so that they can see the value of the profit stream in their hands post acquisition.

In any deal, the Seller will argue for a number of 'Add-Backs' – items which are believed to be non-recurring after the sale of the agency. These can range from legitimate one-off charges, such as the dilapidations charge on terminating a lease, to more debatable items, such as redundancy payments. The Buyer will aim to argue that such items are 'exceptional' but recurring and thus should be kept in the profit and loss for the purposes of calculating the goodwill payment. The Seller will argue hard that they are extraordinary and thus not to be included. Although the relevant accounting treatment will largely determine who wins the argument, there is always room for horse trading in this respect.

Grooming
The phrase 'grooming' is used to describe the polishing of a company for sale, removing all blemishes that may distract or dissuade a potential purchaser. At the core of this process is the regularising of the financial accounts to show a smoothed profit trend in the years running up to sale. To achieve this, the agency must ensure that its accounting policies are aligned with the industry and that any window-dressing of the results for tax purposes is ironed out.

In addition to the list of administrative tasks listed above, it is also a good idea to sharply raise the company's profile in the 2–3 years running up to sale. This is usually done by greater effort in industry awards, more publications, more marketing communications and other forms of outreach within the industry. While this may result in increased marketing costs, it will pay dividends in terms of brand reputation and sales. Although many small agencies pride themselves on their minimal spend on marketing in the profit and loss account, Buyers are not necessarily so impressed.

As part of the grooming process, it is often useful to have an experienced Non-Executive Director join the board to demonstrate good corporate governance and to educate the board on the process of disposal.

Show-stoppers
So what constitutes a 'show-stopper' (or 'yellow flag') as described above? The best method of assessing this is to look at transactions that have 'cratered' on discovery of key facts.

The first concerns a technology platform developer for the advertising industry that was highly profitable. Various offers were duly received and the preferred bidder requested better particulars. As the founder had a healthy mistrust of accountants, he had outsourced all his accounting to a local book-keeper who struggled to keep on top of the figures. Financial reports were usually late and often deficient. This became clearer as the discussions continued, making the Buyer increasingly nervous. However, this could have been managed. What killed the deal was when the owner announced that he was to be investigated by the local tax inspector for tax evasion – effectively he had been running his personal expenditure through the company for years and would have great difficulty separating out what was personal and what was corporate.

The next instance relates to a branding agency. Over the years, they had become very popular with a particular multinational company that had asked them to take on more and more projects due to their excellent services. This had made the agency very profitable indeed, with consistent rates of growth. They were approached by an international marketing services group, keen to acquire in their area. The agency was very open with the Buyer on the extent of their reliance on this major client, which by then represented over 50% of their revenues. The outcome was that the Buyer indicated that any purchase would reflect a relatively low multiple and that some would have to be deferred, due to the inherent risk associated with such a large slice of the income stream. Needless to say, both sides agreed to part company at that stage.

There are numerous other instances of various impediments stopping a sale progressing – usually associated with substantial/unquantifiable liabilities (from aggressive tax planning or long property leases, for example) or structural issues that would prevent integration, such as offices in unhelpful locations. Therefore you have to manage your business in a more institutionalised way in the run up to a sale and prepare for life after disposal, when you will (almost certainly) gradually make way for a younger, salaried management team. A clean, easily understood and well-administered company will undoubtedly pass the test of due diligence with flying colours. If your adviser indicates that you have certain attributes that may get in the way of a successful sale, heed his/her advice and sort it out before starting a formal sale process.

The preparation period will also enable you to get ready for a smooth (or at least as smooth as possible) due diligence period. Below is a checklist for the all the elements of the business that will need attention:

- Human resources: options for key staff; employee contracts for all staff; interns paid minimum wage; PAYE deducted and paid; business transfers and takeovers (TUPE) legislation observed in relevant cases;
- Clients: all contracts signed with minimum notice periods; satisfaction audits available and reasonably current;
- Financial accounts: past 3 years' accounts available (audited if possible); all dividends correctly documented;
- Management accounts: available for the current year; Business plan: 3 year plan available with financial model;
- Directors' remuneration: basic salaries at approaching market rate for one year prior to sale;
- Directors' loans: all repaid;
- Taxation: all tax disputes regarding PAYE/NI/CT resolved and files closed;
- Statutory books: all up to date and Companies House filings in place;
- Intellectual property: documented and secure, all trademarks and domains registered;
- Disputes: client/employee/supplier contracts resolved;

- Property: lease break exercised or lease term to break minimised; dilapidations provided for;
- Software: licences all in place and identified;
- Technology: all developed software properly documented and all rights assigned to the company;
- Data protection: legislation complied with and documented.

CHAPTER SIX:
The approach

'We have to get to know each other before we get into bed together.'
They always said that a good book must have some genuine love
interest . . .

I have never met a dealmaker yet that hasn't, at some point, used a
dating analogy when discussing mergers and acquisitions. It is a cliché.
The further the analogy progresses, the more graphic the language
becomes, so I will spare your blushes. But, like all clichés, it does match
the process with a certain degree of accuracy. I am not going to run
through the entire dating process (you can get that from Mills &
Boon), but I am going to draw on the dating analogy to explain one or
two central rules in the corporate courting process.

*You have to be in love to get engaged: you have to be excited to write out a
cheque*
How many couples do you know who hang around together for years
and years and then, suddenly, you hear that they have broken up and
paired off with new partners? And that one or other has actually
married the new partner within months of the break up? Yes, it happens
a lot.

The same applies to one company buying another: a Buyer has to get
excited about the possibilities of a deal to write out a cheque. They
have to be attracted to the Seller in the first instance (which is why
your public profile counts), they have to go through a period of 'dating'
– essentially chemistry meetings – during which both sides must gel in
terms of vision, values, potential synergies and personality. This process
can take as little as a few weeks, or a few months at the outside, during
which time the Buyer will begin to assess the likely valuation based on

headline numbers discussed in those sessions and the potential market reaction to the deal. If the chemistry and the 'fit' are right, both sides need to explore valuation to see if they are 'on the same page' or 'within touching distance'.

Beware long engagements: familiarity breeds contempt
The second lesson is that it is better, in my view, to avoid lengthy courtship periods. Although there are exceptions to this rule – such as where the Seller becomes a key referral partner to the Buyer – from my experience, 'familiarity breeds contempt'. The Buyer gets to see everything about the Seller, good and bad, if given too much time. They start to see if financial targets are being met or missed, they see the inevitable idiosyncrasies of the business and its setbacks as well as its successes. Like a couple who live together, this can take the initial 'desire' out of the process, which can have an impact on price.

Treating them mean to keep them keen: fear of loss
The third point is that Buyers must, at some stage, fear the loss of the deal. Like a man or woman who sees the object of their desire receiving other admiring glances at the bar, so a Buyer will generally desire an asset more if others are queuing up to take a look as well. This is the basis of an auction; you have to have price tension to get the best deal and that only comes from attracting more than one bidder. You can only manage more than one bidder over a confined timescale; otherwise the various bidders can get out of synch with one another. This causes problems which I will explore later.

You may remember your early courtships (here's hoping they were positive experiences). When you really fall in love or lust, you will remember that you become 'driven' to win the girl or boy of your dreams. It can (and usually does) become obsessive, occupying your thoughts every day; a sort of madness can occur. As a Seller, you want to generate a degree of excitement to carry the deal through the inevitable tricky phases of the negotiation. It helps to create dominant advocates of your deal inside the Buyer (who will inevitably be looking at a range of alternative deals), and it encourages the Buyer to pay a better price for the asset. This will only happen if the desire and the fear of loss peak at the same moment.

I am often asked by Sellers, in our first meeting, if they should 'get to know' the likely potential Buyers in the year running up to the sale. My answer is generally 'no' for all the reasons above and one other major reason: no one likes to see a proprietor 'touting' their business for sale. It can appear subservient and lacking in confidence. Far better to get on with building the business until you are absolutely ready for sale, at which point you work with an adviser to conduct a controlled process. All would-be bidders can admire you from afar – or at least from their tables as you pick up your industry awards.

Time is of the essence

It is worth considering timing at this point, as it can make a lot of difference to the cash flows that you receive from the deal.

As I described earlier, the macro picture for price optimisation is when your agency is big enough to fulfil a 'must have' classification, but still growing at a steady/fast pace to attract a premium multiple. If you are very clever, you will also pick your moment in the economic cycle when market multiples (the price-to-earnings ratios of your stock market-listed peers) are at a historic high, as this will impact on the price that listed Buyers can afford to pay you. But then again, if you are able to predict economic cycles accurately, you will probably earn more money working for a hedge fund than a creative agency. The best you can do is to time your sale during a period of rising optimism, as it will be easier for Buyers to raise capital for mergers and acquisitions. When money is plentiful and risk appetite is high, prices tend to inflate.

The next issue is when in the year you should sell. Most Buyers will want to base the initial price on real, historic financial information that they can subject to due diligence, as opposed to forecasts. They may well be persuaded to pay additional sums based on future performance (Earn-Outs) but we will come to that later. What this means is that in most cases – fast growth, early stage companies being the exception to this rule – the initial payment for the goodwill of your business will be based on an agreed multiple of the pre-tax or post-tax profits for the most recently reported period. Thus it makes sense to aim to close the transaction shortly after the finalisation of your annual accounts, to prevent giving too much value of the next year's growth to the Buyer (assuming that you are growing).

If your deal drags on – this can happen, for a whole host of reasons – and starts to move beyond the middle of your financial year, you may start to feel concerned that the price is based on some old financial performance data. In these situations, you can argue that the basis for valuation should move to the current year forecast, paid in two chunks:

Initial consideration (IC), where:

$$IC = FYP1 \times M$$

and a Top Up Payment (T) paid on completion of the current year's figures, where:

$$T = (FYP2 \times M) - IC$$

FYP1 = Full year profit in year just ended
FYP2 = Full year profit in current year
M = Agreed multiple of profits

That way you can lock in a valuation based on the current year, without the Buyer paying for uncertain amounts of profit in cash on completion.

The fact is that deals get done throughout the year, based more on the Buyers' calendars than the Sellers' (as they attempt to fulfil stated aspirations to acquire in certain sectors), but the ideal timing would be to initiate the sale process at the beginning of your third quarter on the basis of the current year and complete the deal at the end of Q1 in the following year when you have finalised the actual figures. The Earn-Out – if you have one – can then be based on the next 2 to 5 years after completion.

Long lists and short lists

Continuing the dating analogy for a moment, this is the point at which you draw up your list of 'dream' partners, with the help of your advisers. Depending on your size and niche, this can be a very long list or a very short list. Probably the biggest limiting factors are 'ability to pay' and 'reason to care'. If you are a large, multi-office, high profits agency, then you will be beyond the reach of all but the biggest corporations and private equity vehicles which may come from any country in the world. If you are a small, niche player with profits of less than £1m, you are probably below the radar for larger Buyers, but may be attractive as a 'bolt-on' for subsidiaries of large agency groups or smaller unlisted roll-up consolidators.

Whatever your position, there will always be someone out there for your agency; it will simply be about price and deal structure. Therefore, you should consider all possible Buyers:

- Listed marketing services/marketing technology companies (UK and overseas);
- Private equity-backed 'roll-up' companies;
- Competitors that are subsidiaries of listed groups;
- Wealthy entrepreneurs that have sold agency groups;
- Privately owned companies that may wish to merge with you;
- A management buy-out by your senior employees.

Once you have a long-list, you should get your adviser to test the 'buying appetite' of agencies of your type and size. This is done on a no-names basis over the phone or face-to-face. Some of the long-list will count themselves out at this stage on the basis that they are not looking at your segment or geography.

Of the remaining potential bidders, you need to reduce these to around half a dozen, so that you can concentrate the process with companies that are very likely to be interested and potentially good 'parents'. This requires research over prejudice: when considering competitors, there is a tendency to react to negative anecdotal evidence (from former employees) which can be misleading. It is always much better to do proper research into their financial performance and market reputation. The tricky part comes when you need to consider direct competitors that have either lost or won business to you/from you or have poached your staff. My advice always is not to rule Buyers out too early. You may want to have them lower down the list of Buyers, but ruling out direct competitors is usually a mistake, as they probably have most to gain from the acquisition synergies.

Preparing 'the Book'

Concurrent with the preparation of the list is the development of an Information Memorandum, often referred to as 'the Book'. This is the document that markets your agency to prospective Buyers. As such it is a very sensitive document and not to be given away without: (a) careful, no names pre-qualification of potential bidders (by an interview conducted by your corporate finance advisers) and (b) a signed Non-Disclosure Agreement/Confidentiality Agreement in place. Typically, this document will be drafted by your corporate finance advisers and will cover the headline information on your agency:

- Who you are (management);
- What you do (products and services);
- Whom you do it for (clients and customers);
- How you make money (business model);
- How you have developed (history);
- Where you operate (offices);
- How you have performed (financial headlines);
- How you are funded (balance sheet);
- Who has funded you (shareholders);
- How you want to expand in the future (business plan headlines).

Should you include a required price range in the document? This is often standard practice in the US, as professionals in that market believe it weeds out the window shoppers. However, I believe this is an unnecessary statement for an Information Memorandum, as it can result in either lost value (you underestimate the price range) or no value (an over-valuation and no one bids); much better, in my view, to see what the *market will bear* by obtaining verbal or written price estimates following the initial meetings. Buyers will always push hard to get you, the Seller, to tell them what sort of price you are 'looking for'. Always resist this; you never know how a Buyer will value your agency until they make the offer …and it may just surprise you, in a positive way.

Control over the Information Memorandum is essential. It should only contain information that cannot harm the business, so only publicly available (website, directories, Companies House filings etc.) or headline information should be used. Avoid aggressive forward-looking forecasts or detailed business strategies. Only senior management should be named and only client names given that are in the public domain. Ultimately, you cannot prevent a mischievous bidder from sending copies of the document to others (such as the media) but, in the main, confidentiality is generally respected, particularly among the larger acquisition groups. There is simply nothing to be gained in their breaching confidentiality agreements, and huge reputational downside if they are found to have leaked the information. You can, of course, limit the risk of dissemination through numbered documents/'digital fingerprinting', password protection and electronic data rooms (although these are usually used subsequently for due diligence), but none of these will guarantee that you won't suffer from a leak. But it is a very remote possibility if the correct legal documentation is in place and your adviser carefully controls the distribution of the Information Memorandum to a small list of responsible, well-funded and persistent acquirers.

Ideally, the release of the Book only occurs after the chemistry meeting, as you want to get the chance to pitch your case before giving out any detailed documentation. However, bigger Buyers often insist on receiving a document so they can get internal 'buy-in' before engaging in expensive meetings. You should also remember that the bigger marketing services organisations receive countless books and investment proposals every year, so they have to be selective.

Touchy feely time
I am often asked how the chemistry meetings should flow to get the

maximum value. While I don't think the meeting should be treated as a 'pitch' where you wheel out a PowerPoint presentation, it is a mutual sales meeting: both sides need to be impressed. The key is to get into the right frame of mind; you need to be confident, open and enthusiastic. You must leave the room having conveyed that you are on an unstoppable path of growth and momentum. And acknowledge where you need to do better – no one likes a know-it-all. It is also your chance to quiz the Buyer in depth for they need to be open on what they are looking for. Above all, you must like each other, as you are going to work together for several years after completion. However much you can pre-position a selling proprietor for a chemistry meeting, when people don't feel well disposed to such a session, it can be painful. The most surprising chemistry meetings (or even best, in that both sides learned a lot) I have ever attended are – in no order of priority:

- Selling agency proprietor arrives 45 minutes late due to 'bad traffic', leaving his management team to do the initial presentation;
- Buyer and Seller get into a heated argument on the morality of marking up expenses;
- Seller opens up the meeting by saying that she has no intention of working for the Buyer post completion;
- Buyer refers to Seller by the name of a competitor agency (that he is obviously also courting);
- Buyer admits (to the Sellers' chagrin) that international expansion will be nigh on impossible due to territoriality of country managers.

However, in the main, these meetings are uplifting when both sides are open and enthusiastic. Irrespective of the outcome, as a minimum everyone learns something from these exchanges. Where there is a genuine meeting of minds, the Buyer will come back with requests for further information in order to construct an offer.

CHAPTER SEVEN:
Advisers - whom to use and what to pay them

Penny wise, pound foolish

At this point we have to consider the inevitable query: can I handle my own sale? It is the same question that house owners ask when they think about cutting out estate agents. Although I am not impartial on this subject, having sold many businesses, I have also sold companies as a principal and can testify that having no advice usually results in a sub-optimal deal. First, a good adviser, like a good estate agent, will have been approached by multiple Buyers looking for deals – they already know who has the appetite and **what deal is possible in the current market climate**. In addition, they will have done many comparable deals in your sector, and hence they know the price range at any given time. They also know the tricks that the Buyer will pull during the deal process to manage the price down and how to resist these techniques. And finally, they provide the perfect shield of anonymity and calm – 'the steady hand of corporate finance' – which enables you to shop around for a Buyer without impacting your reputation and allows you breathing space at every twist and turn in the deal.

Usually, a corporate finance adviser will justify their fee many times over via the increase in the final price received compared to the initial offer. In new growth markets, where valuation ranges can become greatly stretched due to varying degrees of optimism, this can be even more emphatic. In one transaction, the final bid was five times the opening bid that sparked the auction. In that instance, flying solo would have been a very expensive mistake.

The other point to note is that, in 99% of cases, Buyers will be more experienced deal makers than you, plus they will have an array of advisers briefed to get them the best deal possible (in terms of price and risk limitation), so you need to have a counterbalance.

When it comes to fees, the usual laws of business apply: good skills cost more. In order to conclude a successful deal, the corporate finance adviser will usually charge a low-level retainer to cover expenses and a final success related commission which only kicks in on Completion.

However, you should always seek to employ advisers who are appropriate for you in terms of scale and sector. Unless the asset that you are selling is very substantial, you may find that the substantial up-front fees required by large investment banks will be prohibitive. Also, if you employ an adviser that has a track record in selling manufacturing companies, don't be surprised if the process becomes somewhat scatter-gun.

Lawyers will be needed for legal due diligence, disclosure and negotiation of the Sale and Purchase Agreement (SPA) and all other documentation. They will give a fee estimate for both success and 'abort' (if the deal does not proceed). They may even agree to cap their fee in certain circumstances. But you will be billed if the deal does not proceed. Accountancy advisers are mainly needed to ensure that you do a tax efficient deal and to advise on financial due diligence. The latter costs can be mitigated if you have a strong accounts team in place internally.

Overall, you should aim to control all expenses to within 5–6% of all consideration received. In return, you should expect to get a deal worth at least 25% more than the first offer received, legally watertight and tax efficient. As mentioned above, you will sometimes get a spectacularly better result if an auction can be driven or an advantageous Earn-Out structure negotiated.

CHAPTER EIGHT:
Talking to Buyers: the negotiation

The gentle art of persuasion

The word 'auction' is quite brutal when applied to company sales. It implies that a corporate finance adviser is scanning a sea of corporate faces, taking subtle bids (some of which may be 'off the wall') and banging his hammer down to conclude the sale. Nothing could be further from the reality when selling agencies.

First rule is that price tension only comes from two or more real bidders. Bluffing that there is another bidder never really works (unless you are a champion poker player), because your resolve is far too easily tested by the genuine bidder. So don't attempt it; far better to have your reserve price as the mechanism to lever up the price. Always remember: you own the asset, they want the asset. If talks fail, that is the way it stays and the Buyer goes away with nothing apart from some invoices for professional fees. The second rule is that no bidder likes to know that he is in an auction, unless yours is a very mature, large asset that will inevitably conduct a formal auction. Buyers are not dumb, they will know that you will seek a range of offers; but there is no need to force it in their faces. Thus the process should be formal, but not regimented as this can inhibit your ability to draw bidders into a process and jar with the chemistry sessions. Only if you are selling a large, must-have asset are formal, lock-step processes appropriate.

All Sellers will have their own ideas of value – the 'reserve price' mentioned above. This will tend to relate more to the owner's perception of value than to objective analysis. So the first task of the corporate financier is to provide you with an objective valuation for your business. This valuation (V) should be stated as:

$$V = G + (NCAV - WC)$$

Where:
G = Goodwill (usually stated as EBIT or EBITDA x Multiple)
NCAV = Net Current Asset Value on Completion (adjusted)
WC = Working Capital retained in the business (as requested by the Buyer).

The benefit of this structure is that your accumulated, undistributed profit can be paid on top of the goodwill payment and attract the same tax treatment. This can provide a substantial benefit in the event that capital gains tax (after Entrepreneurs Relief) is applied at a lower rate than income tax, which is currently the case in the UK.

The multiple
The 'multiple' is the number by which your profits are multiplied in arriving at the goodwill element of the purchase price. This can be expressed as a multiple of pre-tax or post-tax profits, depending on the Buyer's preference. I always prefer to focus on pre-tax multiples as corporate tax rates paid by independent agencies nearly always vary from those experienced once part of a larger group.

Unsurprisingly, most of the initial discussion surrounds the multiple, the period to which that is applied (in terms of EBIT or EBITDA) and the amount of working capital that is to be retained in the business. The multiple will vary depending on (a) absolute size of the agency (are you a market leader in your segment?); (b) rate of profits growth (or revenue if you are pre-profit); and (c) comparable multiples of listed companies or valuations of comparable companies that have been sold within a 12 month time period. The latter will vary wildly depending on stock market cycles. In bear phases, smaller listed groups can have low single digit multiples of pre-tax profit. In bull phases, market leaders can attain mid teens multiples of pre-tax profits or even in the twenties for fast growth companies.

All listed Buyers (and larger unlisted) will argue for a discount to the multiple from theirs, to reflect their superior size and market positioning. This is fair up to a point; if your profits are growing substantially faster than theirs, you can argue that such an 'arbitrage' is not appropriate. This is particularly the case when you are delivering a cutting edge service which the Buyer desperately wants. For early stage agencies, the multiple will attach to revenues.

Multiples will vary based on the stock market cycle. For example, the marketing services multiples revealed by the Capital IQ study of listed US marketing services companies throughout the period Q3 2007–Q3 2010 revealed the following average EV/EBITDA multiples:

Marketing Services Sub-Sector	EV/EBITDA Average (Q3 2007 –Q3 2010)
Promotional services	8.1x
Online content & commerce	10.6x
Interactive advertising	11.3x
General marketing services	8.0x
Marketing technology	11.7x
Specialty media	9.8x
Data services & software	10.3x

Industry Insights: Marketing Services, Duff & Phelps, September 2010

These are *listed company multiples* in the USA. If we look at current sentiment in the US market as reported in the Admedia Partners survey (*Mergers & Acquisitions Prospects for Media, Marketing Services and Related Technology Firms, November 2011*) we find that multiple estimates for the acquisition of agencies are lower, reflecting continued weakness in the market and the unlisted nature of most targets:

Sub-Sector	% of respondents	EV/EBITDA Multiple Range
Marketing services	47%	6x to 8x
Digital media	60%	8x or greater
Analytics	54%	7x or greater
Marketing technology	55%	7x or greater
Interactive agencies	70%	6x or greater
Mobile marketing	62%	7x or greater
Social marketing	64%	7x or greater
Custom content	64%	6x or greater

AdMedia Partners 2011 Market Survey (www.admediapartners.com)

This gives an indication of the spread of multiples across the market in the US and analysis of deals in the UK indicates similar trends, albeit that UK multiples are somewhat more depressed as a reflection of the slower economic growth in the country.

Working capital
Most Buyers will want to see that you have left some 'gas in the tank' so that the business can continue to trade without going into overdraft. To ensure that this happens, they will argue for an adjustment to the value of Net Assets to remove items that they do not wish to pay for and then argue for a 'retention'. The assets that they don't want include:

- Fixed assets: they generally don't want to pay for IT systems, company cars and office furnishings on the basis that they will almost certainly be junked during the integration as you move into new space with their IT systems and if you don't integrate, they will assume that these are fully depreciated;

- Investments: non-cash investments, loans to Directors;
- Old debts: anything over 90 days is generally considered doubtful and they will request a full provision;
- Work-in-progress: generally, if work done is not billed at Completion, they will resist its inclusion on the balance sheet on the basis that it is difficult to value.

For most agencies, the issue of fixed assets is rarely an issue, as agencies are generally not very capital-intensive. The valuation of in-house technology development that has been capitalised is inevitably contentious and will require specialist advice. As far as investments are concerned, it is important to liquidate all quasi-cash instruments in the run up to sale and to seek the repayment of loans where possible. On completion, if the Buyer is paying for your surplus cash on a pound-for-pound basis, they will want to be able to transfer that amount of cash out of your account and into theirs to ensure that they remain within their overdraft limit with their lender. As far as debtors are concerned, it is vital to chase cash for at least six months prior to sale, as this is difficult to negotiate away. Similarly, the Completion date should be in the month when you have as little unbilled 'work in progress' as possible.

So what is a reasonable working capital retention? If you are a Seller, then 'zero' is good and is sometimes achieved. If you are a Buyer then three months of trading expenses (excluding re-chargeable expenses) is good. Essentially, this will depend on the cash flow forecast of the agency. If you can prove that you accumulate cash every month come hell or high water, then you can argue hard for a minimal retention. If you have major peaks of cash consumption (such as media payments or bonuses), then you may have to leave a little more on the table. But it is essentially a trade-off.

The negotiation process
Assuming that all has gone well at the chemistry meeting, and that the Buyer has read the Book and wants the business, they will request *additional information* in order to develop a model to support their

offer. This tends to be additional financial information, particularly forecasts. It is important to comply and provide the information speedily, to maintain momentum. However, if they start asking for detailed analysis of client fees and salaries, this should be resisted, as they are crossing over into due diligence, which should only start once you have agreed an offer.

Once they have the additional information, they should make you an offer or terminate discussions. It is always better to resist calls for 'what sort of price' you expect, as discussed above. If you are conducting an auction, you should receive all the offers within the same 10-day time period. It is vital to have all the 'runners and riders' in a line at the outset, for the simple reason that front runners will often time limit their offers, which can squeeze others out before you have properly considered their offers.

On receiving an offer, you should express thanks (irrespective of the level of the offer – at least they want to buy your agency!) and then indicate what you like/dislike about the offer; if you want a rapid conclusion, you can indicate how far off they are in terms of your preferred deal (without naming the exact price target). Again, ideally you will have a range of competing offers, so you can see how the market is valuing your business. Although Buyers will usually indicate their opening offer is their 'best offer', this is never the case – they will be far too wise to lead with their only offer. How far you can push up the price will entirely depend on how much they want the asset and how much bidding interest is coming from other Buyers.

As we will discuss below, the headline price is only one element of a whole range of variables that make up a deal. The top two other elements are (a) how you get paid (what instruments) and (b) when you get paid (deferrals and partial acquisition of your shares). These can dramatically affect how attractive a deal is by increasing/reducing certainty and preventing you from getting your hands on the consideration for a period of time. The Buyer has one central concern: that the agency becomes ex-growth after they purchase it, so that they never achieve a payback. This is the central reason why most Buyers prefer Earn-Outs or deferrals, as they can hold the senior management in the business for a long enough period to ensure payback and integration into the mother ship. Studies by most of the major acquisition groups have indicated that growth tends to persist or even accelerate during Earn-Out periods and fall off quite sharply thereafter.

Negotiation techniques used by the Buyer
It doesn't take Einstein to work out that a Buyer will always try to (a) depress the headline price and (b) minimise the up-front cash paid to the Seller. Even if the Buyer is wary about issuing shares (and thus diluting existing shareholders' ownership of their company), they do not want to see ongoing management receive so much cash that they 'have their swimming trunks/swimsuits on' at the point of Completion. They will want management to stay hungry for a number of years post completion.

So how do they achieve this? I set out below the main techniques that a Buyer will employ to achieve a discount from the market valuation of your agency.

The first (and still the most popular) technique that a Buyer will employ is the development of strong personal chemistry with the Sellers. I have met many a selling proprietor who has been charmed by the Buyers via flattery, exciting visions of the future, beautiful offices and full-on chumminess. Of course this is important going forward, as you will have to work with the Buyer for several years; but you must always remember it is a core skill of the Buyer and it is primarily being used to achieve a 'feel good discount'. So the key is to try and limit the amount of face-to-face meetings with the Buyer until the Heads of Terms have been agreed. Your corporate finance adviser can play a key role here in handling a lot of the initial dialogue.

The second technique used is the Buyer offering to purchase less than 100% of your company on Completion (anywhere from 51% to 80%). This is designed to reduce the initial amounts paid and remove the need for an Earn-Out, by arguing that the sale of the remaining stake is the incentive for you to remain with the business. If you are selling a controlling stake, your objective should always be to have the Buyer purchase 100% of the equity and pay you additional Earn-Out sums based on the increase in your profits after Completion – effectively getting paid twice for the asset. If you do receive an offer for less than 100% of the business, you should still argue (if possible) for an Earn-Out on the percentage purchased up front, as well as annual dividends and the ability to sell the remaining minority stake (see Term Sheet below).

The third technique used by the Buyer is to offer non-cash instruments – usually equity in the acquiring company and/or loan stock. These are designed to lock you into the Buyer for a period post Completion and share in the risk with them, in as far as their share price may in part be influenced by your own success/failure post Completion (unless you are being acquired by a major group). While you should not reject either instrument out of hand, they do increase the risk of the deal substantially. I remember meeting one of the shareholders of an agency that had sold to a listed group in the 1980s in a largely equity-based deal when the shares of the Buyer were at an all-time high; needless to say, they lost 90% of the value of their consideration when the Buyer's shares collapsed.

The fourth main technique used by the Buyer is to seek a deferral of some of the initial payment for a period of time, this being an attempt to use your cash flows to fund the deal. As such it is unattractive; however, if you can get security over the deferred element and the headline price is good, the tax benefits of the deal may make such a technique acceptable to the Seller in the absence of a better offer.

The fifth approach is called 'salami slicing'. This is the technique of identifying accounting deficiencies in the Sellers' books during due diligence and seeking to 'slice' off elements of the profit on which the valuation is to be based. It is occasionally called 'chipping', as in chipping small amounts of value off the price. This can only be resisted by detailed analysis of the 'normalisation' of profits in the Heads of Terms (HOT), agreement on your accounting policies during initial discussions and by an interim audit of the accounts prior to entering into negotiations.

43

Finally, the Buyer will seek to use time as a weapon, usually by time limiting the offer. This can force you to make a decision quickly, before the other bidders can reach that same point in the process. Therefore, resist any 'rushing' by the Buyer; you own the asset, it has taken time to build, so you should dictate the pace at which you sell it. This also demonstrates why you should have all the potential Buyers in the same time frame from the outset.

CHAPTER NINE:
The Heads of Terms

Finally . . . you have struck a deal! An email drops into your inbox with a signed offer entitled 'Head of Terms' or 'Letter of Intent' (LOI) or even Term Sheet (although this is more often used in setting out the terms of an investment in a company). The HOT/LOI will be subject to due diligence and contract and any other conditions that you may have discussed. It will be non-binding on either party, so that both sides can withdraw. What should you expect to see in the HOT/LOI?

In some cases, Buyers like the HOT to be very detailed so that it essentially becomes the front section (and calculation appendices) of the Sale and Purchase Agreement. Others prefer to keep the HOT very brief and focused on the commercial deal that they are prepared to offer. Irrespective of which approach your bidders take, you should expect to see the following elements covered in the HOT:

- *What are they buying? (% of the ordinary shares or the business)*
  This is key; the tax advantages to the Seller of a sale of the company (as opposed to the sale of the business and assets) are substantial and can only be compensated by a major uplift in the price. If a Buyer offers to buy less than 100% of the company's shares, there must be an understanding as to how you can sell the remaining shares to the Buyer and on what formula. Don't accept a position where you are expected to hold a minority of shares in perpetuity (unless you want to).

- *Basis of valuation: profits to be assessed and multiple applied*
  The letter should set out what definition of profit is to be used (EBIT, EBITDA, PBT, PAT, OPAT) and during what period. If the profit used is to be 'normalised' (see below) it should state this

and indicate how the profit will be normalised. The multiple should be stated and whether that will vary depending on performance of the business post purchase.

- *Earn-Out structure and timing of future payments (if any)*
The Earn-Out can take any shape or size and will carry the condition that you keep on working if you are to receive the payments. As you will see below, it is often the case that Earn-Outs apply a rising multiple in the event that compound growth in profits exceeds certain hurdles ('ratchet multiple').

- *Any caps to be applied to the Earn-Out*
A Buyer will always apply a maximum total consideration (initial and Earn-Out total), as this will have to be disclosed to the market if they are listed.

- *Timing of payments*
Payments will be made on agreement of the audit for the period(s) of assessment. If any of the initial payment is to be deferred, this should be stated up front.

- *Split of consideration between cash, loan notes and shares*
Again, this is an essential component and will largely dictate the risk profile of the deal. Many smaller, listed Buyers may offer an even split between cash and shares; bigger Buyers that are cash rich will only pay cash to prevent dilution. Smaller Buyers may also attempt to retain the right to pay the Earn-Out payments in shares if they so choose. This is not generally desirable as the shares may be non-marketable and difficult to sell in any substantial quantity - or in stock market terms, the shares will 'lack liquidity'. The fact is that even companies with market capitalisations of several hundred million pounds can have very little liquidity in their shares, so selling shares may be far more difficult than you are led to believe during negotiations. If you doubt this, have a look in the *Financial Times* at the average volumes of smaller PLCs' shares traded on a daily basis – it will often be in the tens of thousands or less. If you are being bought by a private company, the shares will have no

tradability, so you will be relying on a flotation or a trade sale in the future to realise the shareholding. This may happen, but it will be beyond your control.

- *Lock-in period before agency owners can sell any shares that they receive in the Buyer*
  This can be a very sensitive issue, as the Buyer will not want the constant sale of small packets of shares by their portfolio company shareholders, driving their own share price lower. But to be locked into falling shares is a very unpleasant experience, so this is to be resisted. Shares are largely for the cash flow benefit of the Buyer (although they do help align interests of Buyer and Seller). If the shares you receive rise in value, that is sheer good luck; the Seller will generally want to sell the shares at the first available opportunity.

- *Option to sell any residual shareholding in the future*
  Dotted around the world are legions of founder shareholders in agencies with 20–40% minority shareholdings. Some have done very nicely from the continuing dividends, many have not. The fact is that there is only one Buyer for these minority shareholdings and that will be the original Buyer, so you must have a clear exit path for this holding – at your option – in the future. This is generally managed via a Put Option. A Put Option gives the Seller the right (but not the obligation) to sell their remaining shareholding to the Buyer on the basis of a pre-defined formula of profits post acquisition, times an agreed multiple at a future date.

- *Initial intentions for the agency brand post completion*
  Most Sellers are quite careful about their brand, so some understanding on how to migrate to the Buyer's brand needs to be addressed at this early stage so that there are no shocks.

- *Employment status of selling shareholders post completion*
  Ideally, the HOT will contain a paragraph on the nature of the new employment contracts for the proprietors of the Seller and the likely length of the restrictive covenants post Completion.

- *Requirement for employee bonus pool post Completion*
  Many Buyers may want to see a decent proportion of the agency profit go into a staff bonus pool (typically 10–15%); this is often stated in the HOT where it is clear that such a plan is not yet in place.

- *Any further conditions to be satisfied prior to Completion*
  There may be additional conditions that make the deal work for the Buyer, such as certain client contracts continuing or the ability to relocate into the Buyer's premises.

- *Due diligence: intentions in this regard (scope and timeline)*
  The HOT should contain a brief paragraph on the scope of the due diligence and how long the Buyer feels they will take to complete this. The issue to watch here is whether the Buyer wants to interview key clients prior to Completion; some do and this needs to be handled sensitively. In addition, the need to inspect source code of a technology will be highly contentious and must be carefully organised.

- *Confidentiality notice*
  It is routine for the existence of the HOT to be confidential, which suits all sides.

- *Period of exclusivity required to conduct due diligence and agree a contract*
  The Buyer will seek to agree an exclusivity/'Lock-Out' period during which the Seller and/or the Seller's agent are prohibited from conducting negotiations with any other party. In the event that this condition is broken, the Buyer will seek to recover reasonable costs up to an agreed cap. The period of exclusivity is designed to cover the due diligence and contract period, usually in the region of three months. This is reasonable; six months is not, unless any due diligence is needed on your overseas office network and even then, it is a long time to be locked into a negotiation. The key is to argue for as short an exclusivity period as possible, as this will concentrate the efforts of the Buyer into a shorter timeframe which may help limit

your costs. If the Buyer insists on a Break Fee (see below), it should be mutual; although the Buyer will spend three times (or more) than the Seller on professional fees, you will want recompense in the event that they suddenly pull out for no reason.

- *Representations and warranties*
  In 99% of cases, the Buyer will expect standard representations and warranties from the Seller. If this is to be the case, this should be set out in the HOT.

- *Arrangements on fees and costs and potential Break Fee*
  It is customary for each side to bear their own costs; very occasionally, the Buyer will agree to pick up some of the Seller's costs where it is a very early stage company. The Break Fee is designed to prevent the Buyer racking up substantial costs only to watch the Seller agree a deal with another party. In such an instance, the subsequent successful bidder may agree to pay the Break Fee as part of the purchase price. It is important that this is capped and that you can get your Break Fee paid if the Buyer pulls out for no reason (although they can generally find a reason in due diligence).

- *Regulatory issues (if any)*
  If any regulatory clearance is required before Completion can occur, the HOT should record this.

- *Governing law*
  Wherever possible, negotiate hard for the agreement to be judged under English law, as a dispute in an overseas court could prove very expensive. However, it is likely that an overseas Buyer will insist on their legal system being used.

- *Time limitation*
  In order to force a conclusion, the offer will usually be time limited. This will generally be a creative negotiating technique, but in some cases there may be a reason for their time pressure, such as another deal or the need to announce the deal at the time of their financial results.

CHAPTER TEN:
Earn-Outs

Earn-Outs are a way for the Buyer to secure the continuing commitment of the management of their acquisitions. By setting out extra future payments geared to future performance of the agency, the Buyer can look forward to rising profits as the founders seek to maximise their Earn-Out payments.

In buoyant markets, the Earn-Out can enable the Seller to get paid twice for the same asset if they continue working in the business. Indeed, the Earn-Out can be a massive boost to the total deal value for a Seller, particularly when the agency is still growing fast. In general, they do more for the Seller than the Buyer, which is why many Buyers are trying to avoid them, as they create substantial contingent liabilities that can spook stock markets when the Buyer is a smaller listed company. In most cases, the traditional 4–5 year Earn-Out can be capable of delivering 100% of the up-front payment *again*. But the cost is another 4–5 years of work. Nevertheless, larger marketing services groups that can absorb future Earn-Out payments owing to their sheer scale have found that acquisitions will tend to prosper if the original drivers of the business remain with the company.

The structure of the Earn-Out needs to reward you for this work. As a minimum, it should apply the same multiple used for the up-front payment to your profits achieved during the Earn-Out period. These can either be average profits or milestone profits after each year of the Earn-Out. If you can negotiate it, a *ratchet multiple* (one that goes up if you grow faster than an agreed hurdle rate) can be applied; this can boost your profits even further.

But, inevitably, it carries a number of risks, the main one being that the

Buyer is not in a position to meet the Earn-Out payments at the end of the period, due to the fact that the other parts of their business have not fared so well.

If an Earn-Out is proposed you should analyse it on half a dozen levels:

- Length: do I want to work for someone else for the period proposed? If a week is a long time in politics, then five years is a very long time in business and if you are not used to reporting to a boss, this may prove too much for you to stomach. Make sure you are reconciled to work for the allotted period and that the period is long enough for growth under new ownership to bear fruit;
- Prospects: what are the prospects for the business during the allotted period? You will need to make a judgement on the business cycle and your competitive positioning during the Earn-Out;
- Payment: when will you get paid? Earn-Outs that have one single payment at the end of the rainbow can be dispiriting if trading starts to deteriorate. It may be better to receive milestone payments;
- Currency: how are you going to get paid – in cash or shares? And if it is in shares, at what price will those shares be issued? Sometimes the Buyer will try and issue shares at the same price as at the original Completion date, which can prove disastrous if the shares fall in value, or hugely beneficial if the share price goes up;
- Multiple: Buyers may try to apply a lower multiple to the top slice of your Earn-Out profits – this should be resisted. Indeed you should argue for a rising multiple in the event that your annual growth rate passes certain hurdles;
- Profits: the Buyer may try to tie the Earn-Out payment to *average* profits over the period of the Earn-Out. This will be punitive if you are growing fast, as it will place a 'lag' factor on the profits that are multiplied. But if you are pessimistic about your profits then it may provide some insurance. In some cases, Sellers have been able to 'exclude' the profits from the worst year of the Earn-Out, which is very advantageous if profits are variable from year to year.

What is needed to ensure a successful Earn-Out

Ideally, you want to earn the same again (or more) from your Earn-Out period as you did from the initial consideration; that way you have a tilt at the maximum amount stated in the Sale and Purchase Agreement (thus the phrase 'maxing out'). Hence you are effectively achieving an 'Entry Multiple' in the teens or even in the twenties (total consideration received, divided by the final reported profits as an independent company), which is good going! So how do you go into an Earn-Out equipped with the right tools to 'max out'?

The first and by far the most important ingredient is a highly motivated management team *that is incentivised by the Earn-Out as well.* Earn-Outs are exhausting: you are injecting high octane fuel into your engine and driving it at maximum revolutions for several years. So you need to have others share the burden. To do this, they must have an option granted prior to any sales discussions (or there will be tax consequences on the potential under-valuation of the options) and/or there must be a bonus pool established for their benefit for the period of the Earn-Out.

Second, you need a following wind and/or to get in the big money channels generated by your parent. This can either be a cyclical upswing, a growth product/service or a munificent parent. I remember advising a communications agency in their sale to one of the 'majors' in their world. Weeks after Completion, the parent shoe-horned them into a global account worth millions of pounds annually, with no quibbles on the likely impact on the Earn-Out. For the parent, having a safe pair of hands on a small part of a multi-national account buying £500m of media globally may have cost them an extra £5m on the Earn-Out, but that was small beer compared to the annual profit from such a huge relationship.

Third, you must stay focused on the job in hand. Joining a new group is like joining a new family – everyone in it will come up to you, talk about their problems and ask you to help solve them. You will be asked to head numerous global initiatives that may benefit the Lagos office, but probably not your agency. And you will be asked to join a pitch to

Microsoft in Seattle or Samsung in Seoul or some other monster account that has no allocation of budget for what you do. So always be candid and ask: 'What's in it for us?' A certain amount of back scratching will be needed to get cross referrals going, but be careful to ensure it doesn't run away with your diary.

Finally, you should retain a sense of humour in all dealings with your parent group. The people who you will deal with day-to-day will mostly be paid salaries and will not be sharing in life-altering capital sums that can come from a successful sale. So they may not be naturally sympathetic to your cause! But if you handle the give and take of the Earn-Out with humour and good grace, they may give you the benefit of the doubt in those tricky situations that will inevitably arise. Always remember that – to a salaried manager – there is nothing as unattractive as millionaire agency owners stamping their feet about their Earn-Out entitlements.

Tricky situations that arise during Earn-Outs
You will have to navigate difficult scenarios during any Earn-Out. In no particular order, these could involve any of the following episodes:

- Conflicts: you will be asked not to pitch for a lucrative account as it conflicts with one of your parent's flagship clients;
- Costs: the parent company will invoice you for an expense based on your headcount which you weren't expecting;
- Cash: your parent company will transfer surplus cash from your bank account without declaring a dividend;
- Staff: you will be asked to second one of your key staff to another division of the group;
- New business: you will be left out of a group pitch for a major client which you feel is smack bang in the middle of your area of operation.
- Non-core: you will be asked to take on a time-consuming group-wide role which will be completely devoid of fees.

The tendency is for the Seller to 'reach for the Bible' of sale documentation in order to tell the 'parent' that they cannot do what they are proposing. This is not – generally – a good idea, as it sets all sorts of dogs running and can cause much ill-feeling. It is far better to make the rebuttal and negotiate a concession in return. Only if the action is material to the Earn-Out should you bare your teeth, and resorting to lawyers must be a last ditch, as this will damage the relationship in the long-term (see Disputes, Chapter 15).

CHAPTER ELEVEN:
Due Diligence ('DD')

Why do they ask a million questions?
You may have had a dream like this. You are trying to complete a task –
clearing up a room, running a race, doing some work. But it never
seems to end. The room never seems to become tidy, the race never
seems to end, the work just keeps piling up . . . and you wake up in a
feverish sweat to realise it was just a nightmare. Welcome to the world
of due diligence.

Due diligence is (one of) the reason(s) why Buyers would prefer to buy
your business and assets and not the company; the tax benefit (writing
off goodwill against income) is the other. The past is your problem; the
future is their problem. So the Buyer must dig deep into your historic
trading and current situation to: (a) verify your stated profits; (b)
identify if there are any expenses that have been omitted from the
profit and loss account that will be incurred post completion (such as
underpayment of directors and staff); (c) see if there are any liabilities
omitted from the balance sheet that may come home to roost post
completion; (d) see if there are signs of a fall off in trading (by looking
at your business pipeline); and (e) verify that your technology works, is
100% owned and does not infringe any existing patents.

The due diligence process usually falls into three concurrent processes:
financial, legal and commercial. The financial due diligence may be
outsourced to an accountancy practice, the legal to a law firm; in most
cases the in-house team will handle commercial due diligence, but may
outsource the client due diligence to a market research firm, as they can
be positioned as carrying out a 'client satisfaction audit'. The first stage
will involve the delivery of an extensive questionnaire on each area
requesting historic financial information, forecasts, organization charts,

HR records and contracts, client contracts, leases, statutory books, technology, domain names/trademarks/copyrights, board minutes and all other documents that relate to your current commercial status.

It is important that this giant paper chase is properly staffed at your end so that information is provided in a timely manner. This requires a 'point person' in your organisation (other than you) to coordinate the process, so that you're not deflected from running the business and keeping clients happy. Ideally this will be a key member of the support staff (chief operations officer or financial controller) who knows how to find the relevant information quickly. However, if there is no such person in the business, it is worth taking on temporary help to manage the process. Above all, it is vital that strong levels of organisation are clearly apparent throughout the DD process – leaving long intervals between requests for information and the responses will create an air of frustration and possible mistrust. It will also slow the process down and add to your costs. So it is vital that you manage this process in-house and not wait for an external consultant to carry out the work.

What are they looking for?
In short, the Buyer is looking for anything material that may affect the headline price or require a specific warranty and indemnity in the event that a liability crystallises after completion. There are certain classic areas of risk that they will want to guard against:

- Tax: failure to deduct PAYE on all employees and contractors (where appropriate); failure to account for all VAT; failure to declare staff benefits-in-kind; aggressive tax planning/avoidance by the proprietors;
- Property: exposure to onerous lease terms or substantial dilapidations on vacating the existing offices;
- Employee disputes: potential employment tribunals for unfair dismissal;
- Client disputes: potential demands for repayment of fees for lack of performance; potential loss of major clients post completion;
- Litigation (of any sort);
- Data protection: failure to observe legislation;

- Bad debts: clients that are unable to pay outstanding fees;
- Infringement of copyright: use of unlicensed software/information;
- Loans outstanding: any amounts owed by Directors;
- Regulatory filings: all completed.

As the process continues, you will accumulate several files of papers that answer the queries. These provide the paper trail that will give the Buyer the confidence that you are as you represented yourself. It is important to keep a copy of all the papers provided, as these will be needed to support all the points made by you in the Disclosure Letter.

How to deal with client due diligence
On client due diligence, Buyers fall into two camps: those that won't even think about completing without interviewing the major clients and those that believe the maxim 'what you observe, you disturb' and that it is simply a post-Completion integration challenge. If you are being bid for by the former, you need to consider how the meetings are presented to the clients. In most situations, the cover of 'client satisfaction audit' is sufficient, as long as it is conducted by an external consultancy/market research agency and not (obviously) a representative of the Buyer. If you have only recently completed such an audit, you may have to develop an alternative line. Some agencies feel that this is potentially disingenuous, as the clients concerned will become aware of the ruse when the deal is announced, which is true. However, in my view, there is often little choice - if the Buyer is a listed company, your transaction may constitute price sensitive information which cannot therefore be disclosed prior to the announcement. Better to seek forgiveness than ask for permission. The only exceptions are where the client contract stipulates that any change of control should be notified to them prior to Completion. Even these should only be revealed minutes before the deal has actually signed.

Disclosure Letter
The Disclosure Letter is a key document in any agency sale. Couched in the form of a letter addressed to the Buyer from the Seller, it serves two main purposes. The first is as a source of additional specific information for the Buyer on your agency to sit alongside the

information provided during the due diligence process. Second, it helps to limit the risk of the Buyer seeking reimbursement from the Seller for a breach of warranty (see below). In effect, the Disclosure Letter is the Seller's opportunity to alert the Buyer to anything that might impact on their decision to buy the agency.

The form and format of Disclosure Letters is fairly standard, covering a number of 'general disclosures' and also a series of 'specific disclosures' supported by sets of documentation cross-referred to in the letter itself. Thus it is important to copy all information sent over as part of the due diligence process as it will almost certainly be needed in support of the Disclosure Letter. The specific disclosures are made in response to the warranties in the sale and purchase agreement.

In essence, if in doubt, disclose! By telling the Buyer all the relevant facts about your agency, you are preventing them from making claims in the future if those liabilities come to roost. In the event that the Buyer believes any liability is very likely to arise, they will request a full financial provision for the cost in your accounts. If your balance sheet is unable to support this provision, the amount will be treated as a 'retention' in the hands of the Buyer and deducted from the initial consideration payment.

Conclusion of the due diligence process

So, what is the final output of the due diligence process? If you are given a 'clean bill of health' by the Buyer and its advisers, the various due diligence reports will be tabled at the Buyer's board meeting convened to approve the acquisition. In addition, in the event of significant debt finance as part of the deal, the report will be shared with the bank that is providing the debt finance. In the event that the due diligence process uncovers items which concern the Buyer, these will be raised and dealt with at a meeting with you and your advisers. The Buyer may wish to alter the price based on these findings, which in turn may reduce the appeal of the offer. Undoubtedly, however clean your business may be, a professional team of advisors and an experienced acquisition group will identify issues, the majority of which will be easily resolved. But it is a stage of the process which can derail the transaction if material issues are uncovered.

There is a school of thought that pictures due diligence as a device for 'chipping' or 'salami slicing' as described earlier: chipping/slicing amounts off the purchase price and/or the Net Current Assets as set out in the Heads of Terms, to achieve a better deal. This is occasionally true, particularly where the Buyer has limited access to capital. However, it is not the normal state of affairs for the simple reason that a Seller is very sensitive to such an approach and is very likely to pull out if they feel that their value is being depressed. The due diligence process is focused on identifying aspects on which the Buyer needs protection – big items that could jeopardise the future prosperity of the agency. Buyers that have a habit of using due diligence as a method for price reduction quickly get a poor reputation in the industry and this can impact their deal flow. But where the Buyer has simply identified liabilities that the Seller has not, a reduction in profits and assets is inevitable.

CHAPTER TWELVE:
Sale and purchase agreement (SPA)

Once the first phase of the due diligence is completed – and no material issues are identified that could hold up the sale – the Buyer will initiate the drafting of the core contract, referred to as the Sale and Purchase Agreement or by the acronym 'SPA'. This will be based on the Buyer's standard SPA template as drafted by their legal advisers, with the specific terms of your deal – as agreed in the Heads of Terms – inserted into the document, plus any specific representations and warranties that you will be required to sign up to. The SPA will also contain a list of appendices which will detail any formulae used to calculate the initial consideration and the Earn-Out or deferred payments.

If you are selling a company for the first time, the initial draft that lands on your desk can appear daunting – over 100 pages of dense legal drafting with a range of unfamiliar terminology. While you will of course rely on your legal and corporate finance advisers to navigate you through the negotiation process, you will need to read and re-read the document and its various iterations in order to satisfy yourself on all major points. If all goes well, you should not have to refer to the SPA once the deal is done, other than to check the fine detail of Earn-Out calculations. But in the event of a dispute, it will become the central document for resolution of that dispute.

In order to de-mystify the document, it is worth considering the standard structure. At the head of the agreement will be the named Buyer (which may be a subsidiary company of the Buyer) and the individuals who are selling shares, all of whom will be required to sign the SPA.

(a) DEFINITIONS AND INTERPRETATION

This important section details the defined terms in the document and will contain detailed language for describing, amongst other items, the various elements of the consideration and the definition of profits and working capital that will be used to calculate the various payments due to the Seller. It will also define vital issues such as Good Leaver and Bad Leaver status, which will be extremely important in safeguarding your entitlement to any deferred or additional consideration.

(b) SALE AND PURCHASE OF SHARES/AGREEMENT FOR SALE

This sets out the numbers and classes of shares that are being sold, together with a statement that the Sellers covenant that they are able to sell those shares free of any prior charges ('Encumbrances') and that they waive any pre-emption rights they may have under the existing Articles of Association to buy the shares that are being sold.

(c) CONSIDERATION

This clause sets out the method for calculating the consideration to be paid on Completion and how that amount is to be paid.

(d) DEFERRED CONSIDERATION

This sets out the method for calculating any element of the consideration that is deferred until after the Completion Date. It will generally contain a statement that the Buyer has the right to withhold any amounts due for breach of warranties and deduct these amounts from the deferred consideration.

(e) NET ASSETS AND WORKING CAPITAL

In this section, the method for working out how and when the Buyer will pay for the surplus Net Assets of the company after retaining a proportion in the company for working capital purposes is set out. Typically, the Seller will expect to be paid a percentage of these surplus Net Assets on Completion based on the most recent balance sheet. Immediately after Completion, the Seller will produce a set of Completion Accounts showing the balance sheet immediately prior to Completion. Once these have been agreed, the remaining amount of Net Assets is then paid over to the Sellers. In the unlikely event that there is a shortfall, the Sellers have to repay the balance to the Buyer. Prior to agreeing the Completion Accounts, the Buyer may wish to carry out a full audit, so the top up payment may be delayed by a few weeks or even months.

(f) COMPLETION
This clause sets out the precise choreography and all the conditions that have to be satisfied on Completion, such as changing the company name, accounting reference date, its auditors, directors and the various additional documents that must be presented and/or executed at the Completion meeting (such as stock transfers, new service contracts for the Sellers, bank mandates etc). Your legal advisers will drive this part of the process to ensure that everything is in order so that Completion can happen on the appointed day.

(g) CONDUCT OF BUSINESS
This clause sets out how the company will be managed after the deal goes through until any deferred or Earn-Out consideration is paid. Most importantly, it will detail the basis on which the Buyer can levy any management charge on the company, an issue that is always very sensitive as far as the Earn-Out is concerned. It will also set out any protections for the Sellers by listing matters on which the Buyer must obtain the Seller's permission. The Buyer will fight hard to limit these protections, as it will be their company after Completion and they will want to manage it as they see fit; however, they will be sensitive to the fact that the Seller must feel comfortable that they will not see all their hard work during the Earn-Out come to nought due to drastic changes to the business or the removal of profit through management charges.

(h) WARRANTIES
This section of the SPA is often the most contentious and the catalyst for rising legal fees. The core premise of warranties and indemnities is that the past is the Seller's problem, the future is the Buyer's. Vitally, a Buyer will never attempt to get the Seller to warrant the future. Normally a Buyer will require warranties on all areas of the Seller's operations: ownership of the shares, solvency, accounts, assets, insurance, contracts, regulatory compliance, litigation, employment disputes,

health and safety, environmental issues, IT, intellectual property, offices, and any other aspect of the business. In the event that there is a breach of any of the warranties given, the Buyer will be able to recoup losses suffered by the company (where a breach of warranty can be proven) from the Sellers, subject to an individual claim 'de minimis' amount (usually single digit thousands of pounds), once the cumulative amounts paid out exceed an agreed threshold. So, for example, an individual breach would have to exceed, say, £5,000 before it could be considered and the cumulative cost of all breaches would have to exceed, say, £50,000 before the Buyer could recoup from the Seller.

(i) INDEMNITIES

This clause will identify areas that are subject to an indemnity, namely that the Seller will repay the Buyer on a pound for pound basis if particular, identified losses occur as a result of actions or omissions of the Seller prior to Completion.

(j) TAXATION

The SPA will contain a full tax deed requiring all taxes due on the operations of the business prior to sale to be provided for by the Company or met by the Seller. It will also set out the 'rights of conduct' in the event of tax disputes, which can be of vital importance if there are outstanding issues with HMRC.

(k) CALCULATION AND PAYMENT OF ADDITIONAL CONSIDERATION (EARN-OUT)

The detailed formulae used in calculating the Earn-Out payments will be described, with reference to defined terms for Earn-Out profits. Your lawyers will need to work closely with your accountants on these provisions.

(l) SETTLED CLAIMS

This clause defines when a claim for breach of a warranty can be treated as 'settled' for the purposes of deducting the amount from the payment of additional consideration, or other recoupment from the Seller.

(m) ASSIGNMENT

This relates to the ability of the Buyer to assign the agreement in the event that they are bought by a third party. Some Sellers may wish to negotiate a 'change of ownership' clause which triggers the early payment of any deferred/Earn-Out payments in the event that the Buyer itself is taken over, but the Buyer will most likely resist this as it could be seen as a 'poison pill' by any company that bids for the Buyer.

(n) PAYMENTS
This covers the bank details for payments made by the Buyer to the Seller and vice versa. It will also cover how interest will accrue on overdue sums.

(o) RESTRICTIVE COVENANTS
This is a sensitive area of the SPA in that it defines the period post Completion during which the Sellers are restricted from carrying out a competing trade and/or soliciting clients and staff of the company. The period is stated in years from Completion and generally covers the Earn-Out and a brief period thereafter.

(p) CONFIDENTIALITY/ANNOUNCEMENTS
While the Seller will agree to keep all matters relating to the Buyer and their company confidential, the Buyer will reserve the right to make or approve any announcements in relation to the transaction. If listed on a stock market, the Buyer will be required to make an announcement if the transaction is deemed to be of a sufficient size relative to the size of the Buyer. In practice, the Buyer will want to make a 'splash' about any acquisition in the national and trade media.

(q) COSTS
The SPA will state that both parties will bear their own costs. It is important to note that rules on 'financial assistance' prohibit UK companies from paying any fees/commissions to advisers that are acting on the sale of the company, as this could prejudice the interests of creditors and/or be deemed a benefit in kind. Therefore, while the company can pay for corporate tax advice or strategic consultancy or employment advice, it cannot pay legal or corporate financial fees for advising on the SPA, due diligence or the marketing of the company. These fees must be billed directly to the Sellers at the end of the transaction.

(r) NOTICES

This covers where notices should be delivered in the event of legal correspondence (breach of warranties, formal notification of events). It is important that your legal advisers are the first port of call in this respect.

(s) THIRD PARTY RIGHTS

This enables all members of the Buyer's Group to rely upon the SPA but typically no other third party.

(t) ENTIRE AGREEMENT

This clause will identify the documents that form part of the agreement in addition to the SPA. These will include the Disclosure Letter, possible Option Agreements (in the event that only part of the company's share capital is being bought) and all ancillary documents.

(u) GOVERNING LAW AND JURISDICTION

This states the legal system that will govern the agreement, which will tend to be the Buyer's domicile. This may mean that the contract can be interpreted under an overseas legal system, which could prove very expensive and prejudicial in the event of a dispute. If the acquirer is a UK subsidiary of an overseas group, this may remove this risk (but require that the transaction is underpinned by the holding company).

(v) SCHEDULES

The Schedules will cover detailed tabulations and analysis on all aspects of the transaction, from individual payments to shareholders, warranties, the tax deed, option agreements and the preparation of accounts. This is where a lot of the detailed commercial agreements from the Heads of Terms will reside.

The process of managing the SPA negotiation requires you to remember that your legal advisers – who will lead the process – will need to be managed and instructed. You only want them to fight hard on aspects of the agreement which are material to you or which they believe expose you to risk. There is no point fighting tooth and nail on elements that simply will not be material to you, such as, say, environmental warranties. Where you may be exposed to possible unfair treatment in the future, then you should seek concessions.

The SPA must be crystal clear on how your Earn-Out/deferred payments will work and when you will get paid, as it may well be someone completely different signing the cheque when you get to that stage five years down the line.

One way of managing the complexity of the contract negotiation is to ask your lawyer to produce tabulation of outstanding issues – major and minor - at each draft of the SPA. This will enable you to cut through the noise and focus on the important commercial and legal matters.

CHAPTER THIRTEEN:
Completion

Hallelujah! The deal has completed and champagne corks are popping.

There will be a trillion issues to deal with from the moment that the deal completes. But once the dust has settled, make sure that you savour that moment because it is the culmination of years of blood, sweat (equity) and tears. You and your partners have created value from thin air and…creativity. So you owe it to yourself to enjoy the moment, however fleeting.

Communicating good news

The communication process surrounding the event is a project in its own right and requires energy and focus. In my view your first and most important audience is your staff. As mergers and acquisitions veteran and author of the seminal work *Driving Successful M&A,* Graham Beckett points out: 'The first day under new ownership is unquestionably the most important.'

Staff may well feel alienated by a process that has changed the ground rules of their employment. They are no longer working for an entrepreneurial team; they are working for a large, probably unknown company with a different agenda and their bosses have become wealthy. Some may feel threatened by the possibility of job losses and others may see it as a signal to step up their personal agendas. And the phones start buzzing with calls from head-hunters. It is important therefore to roll out a full programme of communications to reassure staff and educate them about the transaction and the ambitions going forward, without 'gilding the lily' with undeliverable promises of overseas secondments, mega new business referrals and pay rises. They need to know facts and any likely changes that will occur in the near future.

Clients also need to be spoken to, in order to reassure them that it is business as usual. From my experience, clients are (a) too busy and (b) too wise to be greatly impressed by grand talk of additional services and global reach. Such talk will probably send them into the brace position in case of severe cross-selling. It is far better to tell them why the new parentage will be good for your organisation in executing work for them... and that their team will carry on as usual. What does not help is if they read news on a trade website before they get the call, so you should speak to clients before the press release goes out (but while the markets are closed if the Buyer is a PLC). It is also important to check if any contracts have a requirement for the client to be notified before change of control occurs; if so, they will have to hear the news under confidentiality on the morning of Completion.

A useful perspective comes from talking to senior management at client companies on their attitude to the sale of their agencies. The head of corporate communications at a major international company commented that: '...We are far, far too busy with multiple agency relationships to spend much time on such matters. Obviously we like to be informed – particularly if this raises any major client conflicts – and we will put the agency on a 'to be watched' list to check that service levels do not slip. But it's not top of our agenda.'

Unsurprisingly, it is client conflicts that dominate client responses. These have to be identified early on and planned accordingly. In advertising agency deals, they can make or break the transaction.

I am often asked by Sellers how to make the sale an 'inclusive' event for staff so that they can feel part of the process. If planning has been carried out correctly, the key management will receive a benefit from the realisation of their options and an involvement in the Earn-Out. For the remainder of the staff, none of whom have been involved in the sale process, any suggestion of bonuses is totally inappropriate as it does not help the Buyer's agenda. However, I have witnessed transactions where selling owners have rewarded staff through celebrations and other routes. It is a matter of personal style and correct tax disclosure!

Dealing with a new boss

I have never met any selling agency owner that hasn't been somewhat underwhelmed by the attention that they receive from their new parent in the aftermath of an acquisition. I remember one agency owner who having sold to an overseas acquisition vehicle told me that he didn't even get a single call from his new parent group until the first set of half-yearly figures was required.

Although that is an extreme example, it is fair to say that the resources of acquisition-driven businesses are often stretched across multiple deals at any moment and time is at a premium. If the agency is not being physically integrated into one of the parent's offices, then the initial phase of integration will be largely taken up with knitting the company into the financial and management reporting fabric of the group. Thus the burden falls mostly on senior management and accounts staff.

Getting the benefit of longer-term synergies – in particular cross-referrals – is a question of steady and persistent introductions around the group and the development of personal relationships between colleagues. This takes time and all staff should be encouraged to get to understand the shape and capabilities of the group. The process of this type of stand-alone group membership must be led from the top.

If the agency is to be fully integrated, that process is far more urgent and full-blooded. There are many text books on the subject which will explain the need for a rapid and well-planned integration.

Family membership

Many entrepreneurs will have worked in big multi-office groups, so they will have hazy memories of big company behaviour and politics. But every company has its own culture and ground rules, so the learning curve is generally pretty steep. Often, the selling management behave like adopted children arriving in a new family – quite pumped up about their recent success, overly demanding and possibly defensive about their company and culture. This can clash with the more institutionalised culture of the Buyer. It is as well to iron out these differences quickly, so that the Seller can genuinely begin to get benefits from family membership, principally through collaboration.

Collaboration requires mutual respect and good personal relationships, so a degree of humility is essential in the early years. Being complimentary about the parent and responding well to enquiries is a very good start. If this can be backed up by creative and stimulating education on what you can do for the group, the chances are that dialogue will start with all group elements. My advice, having gone through the process of integration myself on more than one occasion, is to immerse oneself in the culture and resources of the parent as quickly as possible. There will be a lot to learn from the accumulated wisdom and resources of the group. However, I would suggest that marketing within the organisation is targeted and well researched, as most members of the organisation will not be capable of referring business or giving you assistance. Above all, with international networks, you only get out what you put in, so integrate!

Ring-fencing and management charges
Having been involved in Earn-Outs and having watched them unfold at client agencies, I know only too well the 'Alamo' mind-set that can be created in the minds of management when dealing with their parent group. In the rush to 'max out', Sellers can become miserly in terms of investment and chary of group initiatives which they sometimes see as unnecessary costs that weigh on their Earn-Out (times the relevant multiple). This is short-sighted, in my view. For a start, the benefit of genuine revenue synergies – which can mean the referral of large amounts of new business if managed correctly – far outweigh the travel costs of visiting your colleagues in overseas offices. Similarly, the impact of positive motivation of the Seller's staff by being exposed to the skills of the entire group far outweighs the cost of a conference attendance.

The key is to ensure that financial ring-fencing – protecting the accounts from the 'dumping' of unallocated central overhead – should not become shorthand for operational isolation. Keep the monitoring of the ring-fence in the accounts department and the board room.

Territoriality

Naivety about multi-territory groups is a perennial. Sellers that have been dazzled by maps with pins in every city during presentations on the acquiring group, suddenly feel like a British Prime Minister at a meeting of the European Union. While one should not be overly cynical about exporting services abroad post Completion, it is worth being realistic. Many multi-territory groups have country by country profit and loss accounts; these are often presided over by highly experienced, well integrated Country Managers who are incentivised to make annual profits and may well hold minority stakes in their operations. They will obviously prefer to replicate your service in their territory rather than import it.

It is important to construct new collaborative models for sharing the spoils in these territories, via revenue shares, joint equity ownership, development hubs and other such innovative structures.

CHAPTER FOURTEEN:
Partial sales and all-paper mergers

Selling part of your agency

In some cases, it may be appropriate to agree a partial sale of your agency, with a significant minority holding retained by the founders/management (typically 20%–49%). The situation in which this may arise is where the Seller believes that the agency will flourish if it is part of a larger group; the resulting synergies will boost revenues and margins and allow them to create a bigger more profitable company, thus making their minority stake more valuable. In these scenarios, the Buyer will want to be able to consolidate the financial results of the acquired business (requiring ownership of 50.1% or more of the ordinary share capital) but will not wish to pay for the entire business at the outset, preferring to retain the original management team, motivated by a significant minority stake. If the Buyer wishes to have full tax planning flexibility for their group, they will seek to purchase at least 75% of the shares of the agency.

Such structures demand that two key elements are dealt with in the documentation: dividend flow post acquisition and the ultimate sale of the minority holding. As far as dividends are concerned, the Seller will wish to be paid their share each year or, at least, to be paid their share of the accumulated post-tax profits on the eventual exit. The Buyer will not wish to be forced by the SPA to pay a full dividend from the subsidiary every year (although they may well choose to do so) as this will reduce their ability to manage group cash flows. Hence the solution is that the SPA must provide for the eventual payment of the accumulated post-Completion, post-tax profits, either via dividend or as an additional element of the consideration for the sale of the minority holding. If this accumulated cash is paid at this point, it may also be taxed as capital rather than income, which could also enhance the returns to the Seller.

The second element of such structures is ensuring the Sellers have certainty that they can sell their minority holding at some stage. The reality of holding a minority share in their agency in perpetuity is generally not appealing. The sale of the minority shareholding can be achieved in one of three ways:

1) Disposal of 100% of the agency by the parent and the Sellers to a third party: this is very rare and would suggest that the deal has not worked;

2) Sale of the minority holding to the parent via a Put Option (see description in Chapter Nine: The Heads of Terms);

3) Conversion of the minority holding into equity in the parent simultaneously with the on-sale of the parent company.

Ideally, the SPA should accommodate the second two points, via the inclusion of an option agreement at an agreed time in the future or at the point of the parent's sale or flotation. The main distinction between the two events is that the agency owners should seek to sell at a higher valuation in the event of a sale/flotation of the parent, for the simple reason that they will be *selling parent company equity* in that instance (even though they are converting their shares into the shares of the parent company moments before the actual cash sale). This is a compelling case for the retention of the minority stake; big companies with higher profits and superior competitive positioning should attract a superior multiple to sub-scale agencies.

EXAMPLE
Let us assume that an agency sells 60% of its equity on the basis of 6 times £500k EBIT plus the surplus working capital in the business on completion of £400k:

Initial Consideration = 400k + (60% x (6 x £500k)) = £2.2m

Under new ownership, the Earn-Out is a major success; EBIT of the agency increases to £750k in Year One, £1m in Year Two and £1.25m in Year Three and the parent company decides not to distribute the post-tax profits from the company (assumed corporation tax rate: 30%). At that point the agency has accumulated post-tax profits of £3m x 70% = £2.1m.

The parent company is then sold at a multiple of 8 x EBIT to a listed company. The SPA stipulates that the agency minority holding can be converted at the parent sale multiple and sold for cash, and 40% of the post-Completion profits added to the sale. This would result in the following second payment:

Second Payment = [(£2.1m - £400k) + (£1.25m x 8)] x 40% = £4.68m

This goes to demonstrate the power of scale benefits and an enhanced multiple, which are the cornerstones of such a partial sale. In the event that the entire sum attracts Entrepreneurs Relief (reducing the rate suffered to 10%), the entire deal will deliver the Sellers a post-tax return of £6.1m for an agency delivering £500k in the year before sale, implying an Entry Multiple of 12.2 x EBIT, which is very strong for a subscale agency.

Minority protections
The main risk of a partial sale is that the Seller loses control of the profit stream – both its delivery and its distribution. In such a situation, an unscrupulous Buyer could elect to manage the profit stream down via various management charges and an unfair allocation of central overhead from the holding company, thus reducing the headline EBIT for assessment in the final sale. Even worse, the Buyer may elect to roll up the agency into another division of the group prior to final exit, making the agency's profit and loss account impossible to track accurately. Thus the Seller must instruct his/her advisers to build strong *minority protections* into the SPA to ensure that the eventual profit and loss account reflects the true trading position of the agency in the years prior to final exit.

These *minority protections* will be built into the Shareholders Agreement and/or Articles of Association that will govern the agency post completion. The Buyer will hotly contest them, as they will be seen as binding its hands as far as the management of the agency is concerned. But without the minority protections in place, the Seller is at the mercy of the parent company board – which may well change during the period of ownership.

'All-paper' mergers

It may be that the owners of an agency believe that they should join forces with another agency of similar size and become one company, without any cash changing hands. The rationale behind such a move will be cost synergies, economies of scale and the ability to grow faster. While such an outlook can be very attractive, these transactions are notoriously difficult to pull off, for three main reasons. First, if one agency is much bigger than the other, it is not a merger but a takeover. As talks progress, this becomes clear and the junior partner in the process realises that there will be no guarantee that they will ever be able to realise the value of their shareholding for cash in the future. The second reason is that the issue of valuation will always be uncertain, as payment is made in unlisted, untraded equity. Thus the arguments over valuation can be difficult to resolve. Even external, professional valuations will be immaterial if one party feels that they are relatively undervalued. Finally, and possibly most importantly, all agencies will have very distinctive cultures, however small. In a merger, these cultures should meld without either dominating. This is extremely difficult to achieve, even with large amounts of integration consultancy.

Thus the circumstances in which a merger can work tend to be 50:50 'marriages' where both agencies are content to share everything straight down the line, including post-Completion management, and where the cultures are very similar. To achieve this, the revenues and profits must be similar and the management teams' ambitions and styles 'sympatico'. Unsurprisingly, these matches are rare; but where they do occur, the task is to keep the momentum of the negotiation going at a cracking pace, ensuring both parties get to work together as soon as possible, so that they empirically confirm their original decision to join forces. Lengthy negotiations and due diligence will almost certainly lead to doubts, loss of the shared vision and 'cold feet' all round the table.

Safety valves in mergers

One of the most important facets of any all-paper merger is to have a 'safety valve' to prevent the lid blowing off the business in the event that one side of the merged entity outperforms the other in the immediate aftermath. If this happens and goes uncorrected, the aggrieved party can become completely disillusioned with the process and seek to return the business to a de-merged state. The safety valve generally takes the form of an additional share award/share transfer in the event that one side outperforms the other in the initial period, or – more usually - that one side fails to deliver the revenues promised at the time of the merger. This is generally carried out by the trigger of a mutual call option or a preferential share issue to the dominant party. It has to be restricted to a very short initial phase post-merger, otherwise it will obstruct the longer-term cooperation between the two parties.

CHAPTER FIFTEEN:
Disputes

Reaching for the 'Bible'

At the point of Completion, your lawyer will press into your hands a 'Bible' of all the documents produced during the deal, led by the SPA. This thick ring binder (or more usually CD) of indexed documents should then go on your shelf and – ideally – gather dust.

The only time you should need to consult the document is when you are nailing down the precise calculation of the Earn-Out payments. At any other time, consulting this documentation could indicate that things have not gone well. If you do have to resort to the 'Bible' it is as well to revisit the legal advisers that took you through the transaction the first time. They will have the benefit of continuity (or should have). Often disputes are based on different interpretations of the SPA, so it is advisable to get a second opinion before quoting sections of the SPA in letters to your parent group. If matters get heated, it is often a good idea to involve your corporate finance adviser, as he/she may be able to negotiate more calmly and navigate through the original Agreement more easily.

The other point to note is that returning to the contract should be your last resort; much better to deal face to face with the parent group management first. Sometimes merely the threat of re-engaging lawyers is enough to alert management to the depth of your concern.

CHAPTER SIXTEEN:
Conclusion

The decision to sell an agency is one of the biggest 'life decisions' that an individual entrepreneur will ever make. If handled correctly and propitiously timed, the sale can deliver financial freedom and the beginning of a new chapter in the entrepreneur's career. Most companies that are started in the UK never sell; achieving a company sale is a great moment. The key is to make use of other people's wisdom on the subject, in books, from advisers and from the public pronouncements of Buyers. Duly armed, you can then master the process and deliver a successful deal for yourself and your new parent.

APPENDIX:
Glossary of terms

A Add-Backs: expenses incurred by the agency that are not anticipated to continue after the sale of the agency and which should be added back to profits as part of the Normalisation process.

B Bolt-on: smaller acquisition where the Seller is fully integrated into the operations of an existing brand owned by the Buyer.

C Call Option: right of the Buyer to purchase the remaining shares in the Seller's company at a pre-agreed time in the future on the basis of a pre-agreed valuation formula.

CEO: Chief Executive Officer

CFO: Chief Financial Officer

D Completion/Completion Meeting: the point at which the sale and purchase of the company occurs, generally symbolised in a signing ceremony and the transfer of funds into the Seller's solicitor's client account.

Completion Accounts: a set of accounts produced by the Seller up to the day of Completion, setting out the precise Net Assets in the balance sheet on the day of Completion; this is used to calculate the surplus net current assets payable to the Seller as part of the consideration; the accounts are subject to approval (and sometimes audit) by the Buyer.

Consideration: the value in cash, shares, loan stock and other instruments paid to the Sellers in return for the agency.

D Deferred Consideration: the proportion of the initial valuation of your agency that is paid after the Completion date.

Due Diligence: the process of investigation into the Seller's operations and financial performance, conducted before the Buyer will agree to finalise the contract to purchase the agency.

Disclosure Letter: Letter from the Sellers to the Buyer setting out all salient details about the operations and financial and legal status of the agency that relate to or qualify the warranties contained in the Sale and Purchase Agreement.

E Earn-Out: the variable consideration paid to the Seller based typically on profits achieved in the years following Completion.

EBIT: Earnings before Interest and Taxation.

EBITDA: Earnings before Interest, Taxation, Depreciation and Amortisation.

Enterprise Value: Market Capitalisation + (Preference Shares + Debt + Minority Interest) – (Cash and Equivalents).

Escrow: Bank account typically managed by the legal adviser to the Buyer, under the directions of both Buyer and Seller in a pre-agreed form.

Exclusivity Period: period of time (months) from signing Heads of Terms during which the Buyer has an exclusive right to negotiate with the Seller to finalise the purchase; generally there is a penalty in the event that the Seller breaches this condition and concludes a deal with a third party.

G Goodwill: the value that a Buyer is prepared to pay for an agency, over and above the Net Asset value of the business on Completion.

H Heads of Terms: An agreement or letter issued by the Buyer addressed to the Seller setting out the main commercial terms of an offer for all or part of the agency.

I Indemnity: An agreement to recompense the Buyer, pound-for-pound, in the event that a specific representation proves to be false, resulting in financial loss for the Buyer.

Information Memorandum: the sale document prepared by your corporate finance advisers for release to potential purchasers.

Initial Consideration: amount paid for your agency on the day of Completion.

IPO: Initial Public Offering of a company's shares on a Recognised Stock Exchange (also known as a flotation).

L Letter of Intent: term used by US purchasers for the Heads of Terms.

Lock-in: period post Completion during which time the Seller is prohibited from selling any of the Buyer's shares that have been issued as part of the Initial Consideration.

LSE: London Stock Exchange.

M Minority Protections: clauses in the SPA/Shareholder Agreement/Articles of Association of the company which prevent the Buyer from running the business post Completion in a manner that will intentionally prejudice the interests of the minority shareholders.

Multiple: The factor applied to your profits (pre-tax or post-tax) to calculate the value of the goodwill of your agency.

Multiple Arbitrage: ability of a listed company to increase its market capitalisation through the purchase of companies at a lower multiple of profits than their own.

N Normalisation: The process of modifying the historic profits of the agency to represent the true picture of on-going profitability after the sale; achieved by re-introducing Add-Backs and attributing market rate salaries to the owners of the agency.

Non-Disclosure Agreement (NDA): Agreement between Buyer and Seller setting out the obligations of both parties in respect of confidentiality

NYSE: New York Stock Exchange.

O OPAT: Operating Profit after Taxation.

P PAT: Profit after Taxation.

P&L: Profit and Loss Account

PBT: Profit before Taxation.

PLC: Public Limited Company whose shares are listed on a Recognised Stock Exchange

Price Tension: ability to drive a higher sale price through the process of an auction for the agency.

Put Option: right of the Seller to sell the remaining shares in his/her company to the Buyer at a pre-agreed time in the future on the basis of a pre-agreed valuation formula.

R Recognised Stock Exchange: a stock market recognised by HMRC as defined by Section 1005 of the Income Taxes Act 2007 for the purposes of determining the taxation treatment of a transaction.

Reverse Due Diligence: investigation into the Buyer's operations and financial performance carried out by the Seller before agreement of the contract to sell where there is Deferred or Earn-Out Consideration.

Restrictive Covenants: Restrictions on the Seller's ability to work in a competitive organisation or approach existing clients/staff of the agency within an agreed time period post Completion.

Retention: amount of the consideration withheld by the Buyer to meet likely liabilities of the agency post Completion; such amounts are often held in Escrow.

Roll Up Vehicle: a company created for the purposes of making acquisitions, usually funded by a Private Equity investment institution or listed on a Recognised Stock Exchange.

S   Sale and Purchase Agreement (SPA): Contract agreed between Buyer and Seller containing all relevant details of the sale of the agency.

Synergies: financial benefits of integration arising as a result of cost-savings or a revenue multiplier effect.

T   TSE: Tokyo Stock Exchange.

V   Vendor: shareholders of the agency being sold (referred to as Sellers)

W   Warranty: a contractual promise (sometimes a representation) from the Seller that certain facts concerning the agency are true and upon which the Buyer will place reliance.

Working Capital Retention: the amount of net current assets held by the agency that is required to be retained in the business post Completion.